MORNING DRESS (1828). See description on page iv.

ACKERMANN'S COSTUME PLATES

WOMEN'S FASHIONS IN ENGLAND
1818-1828

Edited and with an Introduction by
STELLA BLUM

Curator, Costume Institute
The Metropolitan Museum of Art

DOVER PUBLICATIONS, INC.
New York

Frontispiece: *MORNING DRESS (1828)*

Dress of giraffe-colour batiste, with small lilac sprigs. The corsage *à l'Espagnole*, rather high and straight across the bust, edged with narrow cording of lilac *gros de Naples*, and a *rouleau* of the same down the front and on each side in the form of a *stomacher*. It is divided into straps, edged with lilac round the waist. *Sontag* sleeves, extremely full as far as the elbow, and divided by three lilac gros de Naples bands. The rest of the sleeve is shaped to the arm and the wrist ornamented with *vandykes*. The skirt has a flounce half a yard deep, arranged in large flutes, headed by a giraffe-colour band edged with lilac, with semi-circular ornaments above, and a waving band, which entwines each division of the flounce; and beneath are two rows of lilac satin, with orange-colour satin of the same width, cut bias, and placed transversely over the lilac. Giraffe headdress; at the top in front are two high bows of hair sustained by pins and bows of satin and gauze ribbon, interspersed with large curls. Necklace and bracelets of rows of small coral twisted. Lilac gloves, black shoes and sandals.

Published in Canada by General Publishing Company, Ltd., 30 Lesmill Road, Don Mills, Toronto, Ontario.

Published in the United Kingdom by Constable and Company, Ltd., 3 The Lanchesters, 162–164 Fulham Palace Road, London W6 9ER.

Ackermann's Costume Plates: Women's Fashions in England, 1818–1828, first published by Dover Publications, Inc., in 1978, is a selection of 88 plates from *Repository of Arts, Literature, Commerce, Manufactures, Fashions and Politics* as published by Rudolph Ackermann, London, between 1818 and 1828. The selection, introduction and glossary are by Stella Blum, who also adapted the captions from the original text.

DOVER *Pictorial Archive* SERIES

International Standard Book Number: 0-486-23690-0
Library of Congress Catalog Card Number: 78-57822

Manufactured in the United States of America
Dover Publications, Inc.
31 East 2nd Street
Mineola, N.Y. 11501

INTRODUCTION

Ever since they became an institution in the late eighteenth century, fashion plates have continued with unfailing regularity to illustrate the latest modes, and those that have survived have become invaluable records of what was considered fashionable at the time they were presented. Few, however, have been drawn with the skill, style and esthetic appeal found in the early nineteenth-century publication *Repository of Arts, Literature, Commerce, Manufactures, Fashions and Politics*, commonly known as *Ackermann's Repository*, after Rudolph Ackermann, its publisher. It first appeared in London in 1809 as a monthly publication. Although not primarily a fashion periodical, the pages it devoted to clothes were valid fashion plates since they were meant to inform the ladies of the latest styles and to serve as a dressmaker's guide. By the time it ceased operations in 1829, the magazine had included some 450 fashion prints which have since become collector's items. Although the standard of excellence was maintained throughout the years of its existence, the engravings from 1818 to 1828, a selection of which comprises this book, display a unique charm not seen in other fashion prints of the period. Exquisitely delineated, they delight the eye and captivate the imagination. Sweet without being cloying, they embody the new Romantic sentimentality that swept over Europe after the fall of the First French Empire. This volume presents a selection of the best and most representative illustrations.

To understand more fully the evolution of the fashions covering the years from 1818 to 1828, one should pause to examine the unusual times that shaped them. Worn out by wars, traumatic political and social changes, plagued by unfamiliar undercurrents and confused by indistinct new directions, people began to look with longing to the remote past which, with passage of time, had been relegated to the quiet security of history books or to whitewashed and romanticized legend.

With the restoration of the Bourbon family in France, there was a movement to warm over images of the glories of past monarchies. Some artists extolled the virtues of long-dead kings, heroes and historic events. Others gave fairy-tale equalities to classical myths and religious mysteries. Even in portraiture, which had become very popular, the subjects were glossed over with a prettiness so stripped of reality that the original sitter was often hardly recognizable. Idealistic images were sought in every form. The music of composers Mendelssohn, Schubert and Beethoven resounded with passionate tones. The blatant sexuality of the previous period gave way to romantic love, often unrequited and tragic, but always with an aura of purity. In England, writers turned to the Middle Ages. Sir Walter Scott's novels about chivalry, such as *The Bride of Lammermoor* (1819), *Ivanhoe* (1820) and *Kenilworth* (1821) enjoyed immense popularity throughout Europe. The poets Byron, Shelley and Keats emigrated to Italy and Greece, the home of the classical past. Perhaps Byron best summarized the mood of his times in his poem *Don Juan*.

I want a hero: an uncommon want
  When every year and month sends forth a new
    one,
Till, after cloying the gazettes with cant,
  The age discovers he is not the true one;
Of such as these I should not care to vaunt,
  I'll therefore take our ancient friend Don
    Juan——

Byron's evaluation may have been somewhat cynical but fashions fairly reveled in the new Romantic spirit. Although the aged monarchs Louis XVIII and Charles X preferred bourgeois comfort to royal festivities and paid small mind to fashion, Paris still remained the trend setter. New fashions no longer emanated from the French court. Instead, the theater became a source of inspiration as well as a showcase of fashion.

The hard-edged, sophisticated classical silhouette of the Empire period had already begun to melt before Napoleon's exile in 1814. History may seem sporadic in changing but, like fashions, it is evolutionary. It is only the pace that quickens or slackens. By 1818 the earlier figure-revealing, columnar costumes were softened by hem ruffles, embroideries, ribbons, bowknots, artificial flowers and lace edgings. White, particularly fine muslin, was preferred for a few years longer and the waistline remained generally very high until about 1824.

By 1820 the basic lines were almost submerged in ornamentation. The romantic past held a treasure trove of ideas for adorning a lady's costume. From the sixteenth and seventeenth centuries came puffs bursting through slashes and the revival of the Spanish ruff. Collars and cuffs developed points à la Van Dyke and sleeves could be à la Gabrielle (after Gabrielle d'Estrées, mistress of Henry IV of France). Skirts were festooned with roses or made more flaring with corkscrew rolls. Black-tailed ermine became a popular trimming for pelisses (coats), linings for cloaks, and was often made into lavishly oversized muffs. Once reserved for royalty, this regal fur could make its wearer, often a nouveau riche, imagine herself a queen. Fantasy seemed to know no bounds.

The casual hairstyles of the previous period first altered into stylized ringlets, later into elaborate coiffures and finally into foundations for exaggerated hairstyles which utilized almost everything that could be attached decoratively to the head. Like the medieval hennins (tall, conical hats topped with veils), hats grew in size and height. Accessories also became fanciful, with purses shaped like seashells and fans that opened like birds' tails. Jewelry harking back to the Renaissance was worn in profusion. Decorative eyeglasses hung from the neck; watch fobs and chains dangled from the waist. Delicate silks and cottons were replaced by satins, velvets, or silk and wool mixtures. The once-fashionable white and pale tints gave way to strong colors, often combined in sharp contrasts. Children were also attired as though for a costume ball. Little boys were dressed to resemble poets or in outfits such as Scottish kilts while little girls wore miniature versions of the confections favored by their mothers.

To the contemporary eye, the fashions of this period may appear so excessive as to seem unreal. Yet portraits by such artists as Ingres or Devéria and surviving costumes attest to the fact that these fashions really did exist.

Side by side with this extravagant display of ornateness was the other facet of romance, feminine modesty. The rigid corset, which had been discarded during the Empire period, was revived and disguised the natural female figure. The bosom, which nearly had been laid bare in the opening years of the nineteenth century, was chastely covered and concealed under layers of trimmings, though still placed high. It even became fashionable to veil the arms, which might be exposed by the short sleeves of evening dresses, with transparent oversleeves of aerophane (a thin crepe). The coif and wimple, hallmarks of uxorial constancy in the past, found expression in pretty frilly caps that had little to do with the marital state of the wearer and were worn as house caps and sometimes out-of-doors under hats particularly under bonnets, which originated in this period and grew to become the symbol of feminine decorum during most of the nineteenth century.

This was an age that sought escape through enchantment and through metaphoric poetry. Looking at the wistful doll-like creatures, so charmingly portrayed in the Ackermann prints—these maidens with their eyes cast downward in modesty or upward in innocence—one somehow gets the feeling their feet barely touched the ground of reality. This was a transitional period, a period of searching, in which one can observe the demise of an old fashion and the development of a new one. It shows how, beginning with such small details as a decoration on a hem or sleeve, the spirit of a style becomes altered and continues to grow in a new direction until something new emerges with only a few minor vestiges of the old remaining. By 1828 the age of Josephine and her circle was gone and, although Victoria was only nine years old and would not be queen for nine more years, the seeds of the Victorian era had already been sown.

The captions accompanying the plates have been taken, with minor changes, from the originals in *Ackermann's*. Words appearing in *italics* are defined in the Glossary, page 88. Sixteen plates have been reproduced in full color and can be found following page 26.

WALKING DRESS (1818)

A *round dress* composed of thin *jaconet* muslin, over a pale peach-coloured *sarsnet* slip: the body of the gown is made high, and is trimmed with triple fall of lace at the throat. The bottom of the skirt is flounced with rich *French work*, which is surmounted by a *rouleau* of muslin and this rouleau is headed by fancy trimming. The *spencer* worn with this dress is composed of white striped *lutestring*; the fronts are richly ornamented with braiding. The headdress, a leghorn hat, the brim large, and turned up behind in a soft roll in the French style; the crown is ornamented with four rouleaux of peach-coloured satin twined with white cord. White kid shoes, and straw-coloured gloves.

1

EVENING DRESS (1818)

A black *crape* frock over a black *sarsnet* slip: the body is composed of white crape tastefully ornamented with deep *vandykes* of black velvet; each vandyke finished at the point by a little light ornament of black chenille. Short full sleeves of intermixed black and white crape; fulness drawn to the middle of the arm, confined in three separate folds by vandykes of black velvet. The bottom of the skirt is finished by a row of black velvet vandykes, surmounted by a large *rouleau* of white crape, entwined with black chenille; two rows of roses, com-posed of black crape mixed with chenille complete the trimming. Headdress, a white crape *toque,* is ornamented around the front in chenille and finished by a diadem of white crape roses. Earrings, armlets, necklace and cross composed of jet. Black *chamois* leather gloves and slippers which are ornamented with rosettes of white chenille. A black China crape scarf, richly worked at the ends in an embroidery of white flowers, is finished by a black silk fringe.

CARRIAGE DRESS (1818)

Bombasine high dress: the body is quite plain. The skirt is trimmed around the bottom with double row of black *crape*. This is surmounted by a row of *Spanish puffs*. Over this is a *rouleau* of intermingled black crape and rich black silk trimming and above is placed a row of somewhat smaller Spanish puffs. With this dress is worn the Russian wrapping-cloak composed of mole-skin cloth and lined with black *sarsnet*. A *pelerine* of enormous size, and a full hood render this a most comfortable envelope. Parisian bonnet has a crown of moderate height; the brim has an edge finished by a full band of crape, and crape roses set on at small distances: it is ornamented with a wreath of black flowers. Morning *cornette* composed of thin long lawn, the borders edge in black. Black *chamois* leather sandals and gloves. *Reticule,* composed of black velvet at the corners with white silk tassels and a rich white silk trimming around the top.

3

WALKING DRESS (1818)

An open robe composed of *jaconet* muslin and trimmed with *mull* muslin laid on full; the fulness is drawn in by welts. The body is made tight to the shape, and has a collar welted to correspond to the trimming. Over this robe is worn a *spencer*, composed of a new material, of a beautiful pale canary colour. The bust is slightly ornamented with evening primrose satin. The shoulder is very tastefully finished with full puffs of satin, each fastened down by a button of the same colour. The spencer comes up to the throat, and the collar of the dress falls over. The headdress is a French bonnet, of the same material, finished at the edge of the brim with primrose satin; a bunch of flowers and an elegant plume of ostrich feathers are placed on one side. Gloves and shoes, pale canary color.

4

WALKING DRESS (1818)

A *round dress* of *jaconet* muslin; a frill of rich work stands around the throat, and goes down the fronts. The bottom of the skirt is finished by a flounce of work disposed in large *plaits*; this is surmounted by a row of embroidery and a second flounce of work, over which are three or four welts. The *spencer* is composed of dark blue *Gros de Naples*; it is made tight to the shape, without seam, and richly ornamented with white satin. The collar, which stands up round the throat is composed of white satin: it is very full, but the fulness is confined by narrow bands of Gros de Naples; small white tassels depend from each band. Headdress, a *cornette* of white lace ornamented by bias bands of white satin. The top of the crown is full; the fulness is confined by a wreath of moss-roses. Bonnet of a French shape, composed of white satin, the edge of the brim finished by *rouleaux* of blue and white plaid silk; a large bow of same material, and a plume of ostrich feathers, are placed on one side of the crown. White gloves, and half-boots, the lower part blue leather, the upper part *jane*. A lemon-coloured shawl, very richly embroidered, is thrown loosely over the shoulders.

WALKING DRESS (1818)

A *round dress* of black *bombasine*; the body is made tight to the shape and up to the throat, but without a collar; the skirt is finished at the bottom with a broad black *crape* flounce; over this is a very narrow flounce, which is *quilled* in the middle to correspond, and the whole is surmounted by a broad band of bias crape. The *spencer* is composed of black cloth; it is cut without a seam, and ornamented with a fulness of black crape, disposed in large *plaits* at the bottom of waist; a high standing collar rounded in front is edged with a light trimming of black crape; long loose sleeves have epaulettes draperied with black cord and ornamented with small tassels. Headdress, a bonnet of black crape; the edge of brim is finished with a row of large hollow plaits. A white crape frill stands up round the throat. Gloves and shoes of black *chamois* leather.

6

RIDING DRESS (1818)

A habit composed of fine slate-coloured cloth; the skirt is of moderate fulness and finished up the front with braiding. Headdress, a small round hat composed of cork. Slate-coloured leather boots and *Limeric* gloves.

7

EVENING DRESS (1818)

A blue satin slip, over which is a British net frock: the body is cut very low all round the bust; and the waist, which is extremely short, is ornamented, in the French style, with a row of *blond* set on full at the bottom. The sleeve is short and is decorated with knots of blue ribbon. The skirt is made more than usually full; is trimmed with a deep flounce of rich blond lace, which is intermingled with branches of grape-blossoms, and surmounted by a row of satin cockle-shells which are connected by a narrow *rouleau* of satin. Headdress, the Kent *toque*, composed of Parisian gauze of a bright yellow color, embroidered in small roses. Necklace and earrings are composed of sapphires. White kid gloves and white satin shoes.

EVENING DRESS (1818)

A white lace dress over a white satin slip; the bottom of the skirt is trimmed with a drapery of white lace entwined with pearl and ornamented with full-blown roses which are placed at regular distances; a *rouleau* of white satin is placed above and another below. *Corsage* of pale rose-coloured satin, made tight and cut so as to display the bust very much; a row of blond lace is set on plain so as to fall over the corsage. Short full sleeve of rose satin, slashed with white lace, and finished at the bottom by a fall of *blond* set on plain. Headdress, a white satin *toque*, made rather high and ornamented with a bunch of flowers at the left side. White kid gloves. Necklace and earrings, pearl. Hair arranged in a few light ringlets on each temple. Small ivory fan.

9

EVENING DRESS (1818)

A black *crape* dress over a black *sarsnet* slip. The body is cut very low and square around the bust, and is tight to the shape. It is trimmed round the bosom and the back with a *rouleau* of crape intermixed with jet beads. The bottom of the waist is finished by rounded tabs. Long sleeve, made very loose, is disposed on the shoulder in puffs, which are interspersed with jet beads, some of which also confine it across the arm: this forms a new and elegant style of half-sleeve. The bottom of the skirt is cut in broad scallops the edges of which are ornamented with narrow black fancy trimming, and an embroidery of crape roses. The front hair is much parted on the forehead, and disposed in light loose ringlets, which fall over each ear. The hind hair is braided, and brought round the crown of the head. Headdress, a long veil and an elegant jet ornament consisting of a rose and an *aigrette*. *Chamois* leather gloves and shoes. Earrings, necklace and cross, jet.

10

EVENING DRESS, HALF MOURNING (1819)

A white *crape round dress* over a white *sarsnet* slip; it is cut very low all round the bust, and the waist is as short as possible; a full sleeve which is likewise very short. The bottom of the skirt is ornamented with a full *rouleau* of white crape, which stands out, and is surmounted by a broad trimming of jet beads. A white crape apron is worn with this dress, it is a three-quarter length, narrow at the top, and broad towards the bottom; it is finished with rich tassels at each end, and has a slight embroidery in black all round. A necklace and brooch of jet, put on in the Grecian style, partly shade the bust. Earrings, armlets, and bracelets of jet to correspond. Headdress, la *toque de Ninon*, is ornamented with a long plume of ostrich feathers which fall over to the left side, and a butterfly of jet is placed in the centre of the forehead. White leather shoes with jet clasps. White kid gloves.

11

WALKING DRESS (1819)

A high dress composed of French grey *Circassian cloth*: the bottom of the skirt is ornamented with bands of white *lutestring*, edged with cord the colour of the dress which forms lozenges; each lozenge is ornamented at the top and bottom with a white lutestring rose. The body is made up to the throat, but without a collar; it is ornamented round the top of the bust with a light silk trimming; both the back and front are full but the *Athenian braces* which are worn with it, confine it to shape. These braces are composed of white lutestring and have a very full epaulette. The headdress is a French walking hat, in shape something similar to a gentleman's. It is composed of plain straw-coloured silk *pluche*; the crown is oval; the brim is formed into an oval shape by being turned up in a soft roll on each side. The edge of the brim is ornamented with slate-coloured satin twisted to form what the French call a *torsade*. A long plume of white ostrich feathers with curled edges is placed on one side. French grey gloves. Half-boots, the upper part French grey silk, the lower part black leather. A large India scarf is thrown over the shoulders. This dress is worn as a carriage costume as well as for an elegant promenade dress.

WALKING DRESS, HALF MOURNING (1819)

A *round dress* of figured silk, the ground grey, with a small black leaf. The body is made partially high round the shoulders and back but sloped low in front; it is trimmed with a puffing of grey *crape*, ornamented between each puff with a jet bead. The bottom of the skirt is trimmed with a deep flounce of black crape, embroidered in grey silk: this is surmounted by a plain band of black crape embroidered in grey silk, and the whole is finished by a broad band of bias black satin laid on full. *Fichu* of white crape with a very full ruff. Over this is a *pelisse* composed of either black or grey velvet, lined with white *sarsnet*.

The body is made tight to the shape and comes up high behind but has no collar; it is sloped in front so as to display the fichu; it wraps across the front and has a falling white satin *pelerine*. The sleeve is tight; the shoulders are finished by puffings of white satin. The trimming, which goes all round the pelisse, consists of satin *coquings*, interspersed with leaves. Headdress a gypsy hat, composed of British *Leghorn*, and ornamented with full plume of ostrich feathers; the brim is turned up before and behind. Black leather half-boots. White kid gloves. Ermine muff.

13

MORNING DRESS (1819)

A *round dress* composed of *jaconet* muslin; the skirt is full, and trimmed at the bottom with a piece of muslin drawn into six *easings* with pink ribbon; a row of buttons is placed above them, and is surmounted by three easings to correspond. The body is high. There is a small collar and a *pelerine* affixed to it; it is double: the lower is rounded trimmed with two rows of easings, and edged with narrow lace; the upper part is pointed and trimmed to correspond. The back is plain and fastens behind; a low front is attached to the high one; the former

disposed in small *plaits* across, is laced up before with cord and buttons, and is trimmed with a single row of easing and narrow lace. Long loose sleeve, finished with easings to correspond. Headdress, the *Parisian mob*. It has small ears and does not come quite close under the chin where it ties with a pink ribbon; it is ornamented with a garland of exotics. The hair is dressed in light ringlets on the forehead. Rose-coloured slippers, and *Limeric* gloves.

WALKING DRESS (1819)

A *jaconet* muslin petticoat, ornamented round the bottom with four rows of muslin trimming composed of narrow welts finished with edging. Over this is an open robe worked all round in a very rich and elegant pattern. The *spencer* worn with this dress is composed of green *gros de Naples*; the bust is displayed to advantage by a small *plaited* front attached to the high one; the former fastens before with an ornamental clasp. Plain back. The collar, epaulettes and cuffs are richly braided, and the edges of each finished by a light chain of braiding. Headdress, a hat composed of cork; it is intermixed with green satin, and lined with the same material: the crown is of a moderate size; the brim is the same width all round; it is ornamented with a plume of feathers; a small *cornette* with a double border of pointed lace is worn underneath. *Limeric* gloves and green shoes.

15

CARRIAGE DRESS, MOURNING (1820)

A loose wrapping-coat of very fine black cloth worn over a black *bombasine* dress. The coat is lined and trimmed with ermine. The *pelerine*, collar and cuffs are also of ermine. A white *crape fichu*, with a full puckered collar, tied with a black *love ribbon*, shades the bust of the dress and stands above the collar of the coat. Headdress, a bonnet composed of black crape over black *sarsnet*: the crown is ornamented with twisted *rouleaux* of black crape, placed crosswise; the brim is lined with double white crape; a black feather ornament is placed in front, and a full bow of crape ties it under the chin. Black *chamois*-leather half-boots and gloves.

16

WALKING DRESS (1819)

A *pelisse* composed of *kerseymere*. The colour is a peculiar shade of grey; it is lined with white *sarsnet*. The sleeve is wide and falls very much over the hand. The skirt is moderately full, meets before and fastens down on the inside. The trimming is composed of ruby-coloured velvet; it goes round the bottom and up each of the fronts. The epaulettes and cuffs correspond with the trimming. High standing collar trimmed in a similar manner. Headdress, a bonnet composed of ruby velvet, intermixed with *levantine*: the crown is made of folds of these two materials so disposed as to form a point in the centre; the brim is large and is finished at the edge by a rich roll of ruby levantine to which is attached a full fall of blond lace, set narrow towards the ears and broad in the middle of the brim. A high plume of ostrich feathers is placed upright in front. Gloves to correspond with the pelisse. Half-boots, the lower part of black leather, the upper part of grey levantine.

17

CARRIAGE DRESS (1820)

A round dress, composed of French grey *bombasine* and trimmed with black gauze which is disposed on the skirt in rows of full *plaits*, which are laid on lengthwise in a bias direction. Each row of plaits is edged with black satin ribbon. The body is made high. The collar stands out a little from the neck; it is peaked in the centre back, and slopes down so as just to meet in front. The long sleeve is ornamented by three black satin *rouleaux*, and finished at the hand by a full fall of white crape, scalloped at the edge. The half sleeve is made very full; the fullness is divided into compartments by narrow rouleaux of black satin. A very full ruff is partially seen under the collar. Headdress, a bonnet composed of grey *velours simulé*, and lined with white *sarsnet* the edge of the brim is finished by a full black gauze *ruche*; a bunch of black flowers is placed on one side of the crown, and it ties under the chin with black strings. Grey kid gloves and black kid half-boots.

18

WALKING DRESS (1820)

The *pelisse* is composed of fine black cloth; the back is plain at the top, but has a little fulness at the bottom at the waist. The trimming consists of three bands of black *crape* cut bias and doubled; they are of different widths, and are set on at a little distance from each other. Headdress, a *cornette* composed of white crape, and a bonnet of black crape over black *sarsnet*. The crown is round; the brim is lined with white crape dou-bled and is finished at the edge by a deep fall of black crape. A full bunch of roses of the same material is placed at one side of the crown, which is encircled by a plain band of black crape; another band confines it under the chin. The ruff is of white crape and very full. Black leather half-boots and *chamois* gloves.

WALKING DRESS (1820)

The *pelisse* is composed of the beautiful new silk called *zephyrine*; the colour is a peculiar shade of lavender. It is made tight to the shape and ornamented with rosettes on the hips, and has a high collar rounded in front. The sleeve is finished at the hand by three narrow *rouleaux* of *gros de Naples,* each at a little distance from the other. The half-sleeve is composed of alternate folds of gros de Naples and zephyrine. The skirt is of an easy fulness and is trimmed at the bottom only with a fulness of lavender-coloured gauze, intermixed with satin to correspond. Headdress, a bonnet composed of white gros de Naples. The crown is low; the brim large, formed something in the *capuchin* style, but to stand out a good deal from the face. The edge of the brim is finished with *blond,* and a bouquet, composed of a full-blown rose, surrounded with buds and leaves, is placed in front. Strings, to correspond with the pelisse, tie it under the chin. Lavender-coloured kid boots, and *Limeric* gloves.

EVENING DRESS, MOURNING FASHION
(1820)

A black *crape round dress*, over a black *sarsnet* slip: the corsage is cut very low all round the bust. A *pelerine* of white crape is affixed to the back, and comes down on each side of the bust as low as the waist in front. It consists of four falls of double puckered crape; is rounded behind, and pointed at the fronts. The bottom of the skirt is ornamented with a broad trimming of white crape; intersected with narrow *coquings* of black crape, disposed in a scroll pattern. There are two rows of these laid on the white crape, at some distance from each other. Headdress, a *demi-cornette,* composed of white crape, over which is a small crape hat. The brim is of equal breadth all round, but is bent down a little in back. It is lined with white crape, and trimmed with a full puffing of the same material round the edge of the brim. Three white feathers decorate the crown. Necklace and earrings, jet. Black *chamois* leather gloves and shoes.

EVENING DRESS (1820)

A *round dress*, composed of *Urling's net*, over a white satin slip. The dress is gored and sufficiently full to hang in easy folds round the figure. The bottom of the skirt is trimmed with flounces of Urling's lace, headed by *rouleaux* of white *zephyrine*. These flounces are festooned with bouquets of roses and blue-bells. The *corsage* is tight to the shape and ornamented with lozenges of net, each lozenge formed by a large pearl. The sleeve is very short. It is composed of fulness of net over white satin, interspersed with pearls laid on in waves; the bottom of the sleeve is finished by a twisted *rouleau* of satin and pearls. Hair dressed in the French style, in a profusion of full curls which are brought very low at the sides of the face. The hind hair is brought up in full bows on the crown of the head and partly concealed by a garland of roses. Earrings, and necklace, pearls. White satin slippers, and white kid gloves.

COURT DRESS (1820)

A blue satin petticoat finished at the bottom by a silver foil trimming, above which is a mingled wreath of white and pale bluish roses. This is surmounted by a rich trimming of silver lamé. Over the blue satin petticoat is one of point lace, short enough to display the entire of the rich trimming of the satin petticoat. The border of lace has a pattern in the middle of roses, thistle and shamrock entwined. The *corsage* is white satin, and the front, which is formed in the *stomacher* style, is nearly covered with pearls. The robe is blue *zephyrine*; the body rather long in the waist; the back part made corset style. The robe is trimmed round with *Urling's point lace*, set on very full. The sleeve is white satin, covered with *blond lace* intermixed with pearls. The front hair is disposed in few light ringlets on the forehead; the hind hair is concealed by a profusion of ostrich feathers which is encircled by a broad pearl *bandeau*. Point lace *lappets*, white kid gloves and white satin shoes, ornamented with rosettes of pearl. Necklace and earrings, pearl. White *crape* fan richly embroidered in silver.

BALL DRESS (1820)

A slip composed of pale pink satin, finished at the bottom with a light wreath of artificial cornflowers mixed with ears of ripe wheat. This is surmounted by a trimming composed of pearl embroidered in ornaments which resemble the shape of the prince's [Prince of Wales] plume. The robe is composed of white lace; it is open on the left side, is edged with pearls, and is looped all round with knots of pearl and bouquets of fieldflowers which are placed alternately. The *corsage* tight to the shape is a little peaked behind. The bust is ornamented with a *stomacher* composed of pink satin, richly decorated with pearls. A little bouquet of roses ornaments the left shoulder. Short sleeves, composed of white lace over pink satin are slashed in the Spanish style. The headdress is composed of flowers: a wreath of roses placed low on the forehead is surmounted by a half-garland composed of fancy-flowers placed on the crown of the head. Necklace, earrings, pearl. White kid gloves, and white corded silk shoes.

EVENING DRESS (1820)

A *round dress* composed of white *crape*, spotted with white satin. It is worn over a white *sarsnet* slip. The skirt is finished at the bottom by a wreath of flowers and leaves composed of black silk. The flowers, which are roses, are very small; a double row of leaves, placed thickly together, with points downwards, is attached to them. The *corsage* is composed of black *velours simulé*: the waist is long, and it is a little, but very little, peaked in front, and it fastens behind. The upper part of the body is composed of white crape, let-in in easy folds, and confined in the centre of the bosom by a jet clasp. Short full sleeve; the upper part composed of velours simulé, edged with white crape trimming and fastened up in the drapery style. The under sleeve is white crape finished by a pointed fall. The front hair is dressed in light ringlets; the hind hair is disposed in different *plaits*, which are fastened up in bows. White flowers, intermixed with pearls fancifully disposed, ornament the hair. The necklace and earrings are also pearl. White kid gloves and shoes.

COTTAGE DRESS (1820)

A *round dress* composed of drab-coloured *bombasine*. The skirt, of a moderate width, is finished at the bottom by a full *plaiting* of peach-coloured satin ribbon above which is a trimming of the same material arranged in puffs of different forms, which are placed alternately. The bust is ornamented with twisted band of white and peach-coloured satin. A peasant's apron of the same material as the gown finishes the dress. It is trimmed with a narrow *rouleau* of peach-coloured satin laid on in waves; the point of each wave is finished by a satin rosette to correspond. The bust is partially shaded by a peach-coloured handkerchief, which is tied carelessly round the throat. Head-dress, a cottage hat: crown resembles a man's. The brim is of moderate size, broader in front than behind and bent down a little over the forehead. The brim and the top of the crown have a slight edging of peach-coloured satin. A band of ribbon to correspond encircles the bottom of the crown; a full bow is placed on one side, and strings fasten under the chin.

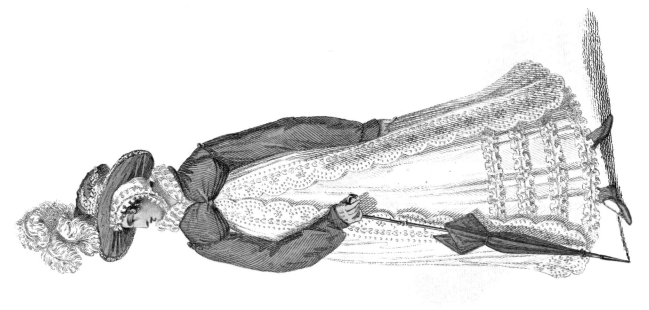

WALKING DRESS (1819)
For description, see page 15

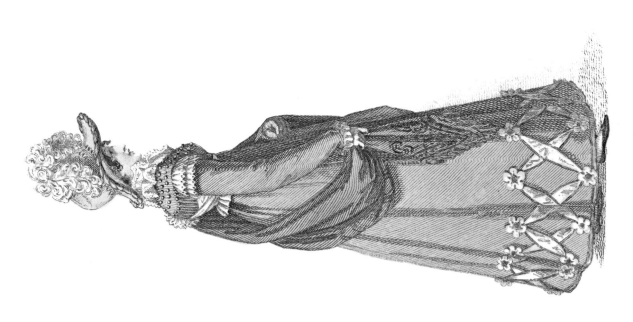

WALKING DRESS (1819)
For description, see page 12

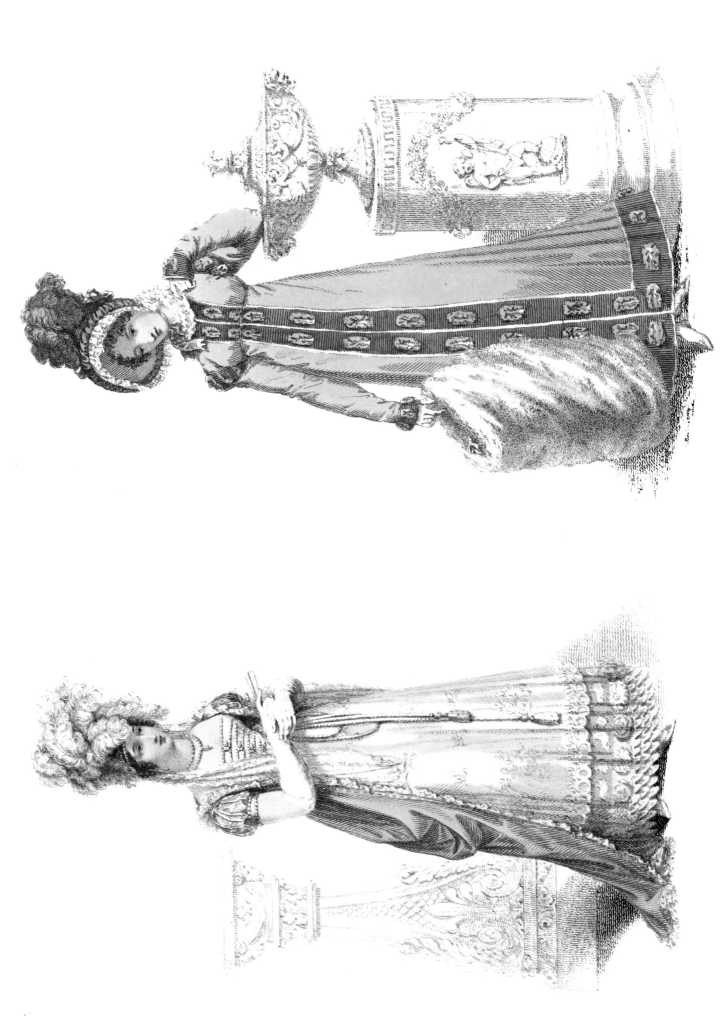

WALKING DRESS (1819)
For description, see page 17

COURT DRESS (1820)
For description, see page 23

MORNING DRESS (1824)
For description, see page 44

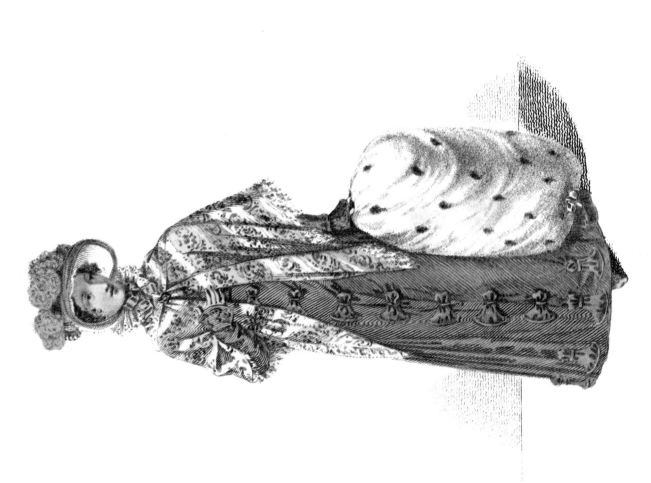

PROMENADE DRESS (1821)
For description, see page 34

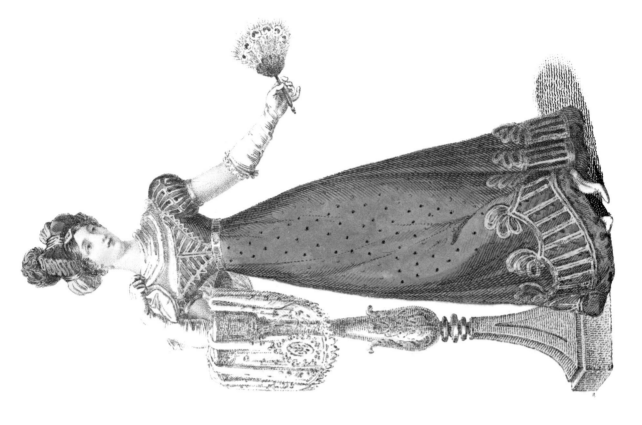

FULL DRESS (1823)
For description, see page 43

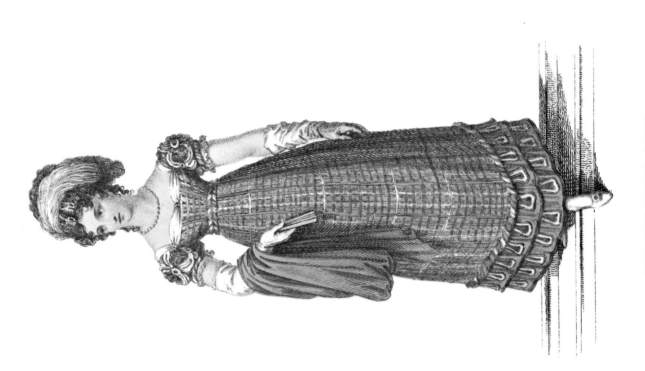

EVENING DRESS (1822)
For description, see page 38

WALKING DRESS (1826)
For description, see page 67

PROMENADE DRESS (1824)
For description, see page 42

BALL DRESS (1826)
For description, see page 68

DINNER DRESS (1826)
For description, see page 69

CARRIAGE DRESS (1827)
For description, see page 80

PROMENADE DRESS (1827)
For description, see page 73

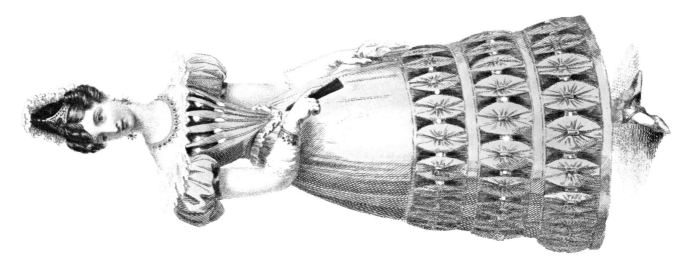

BALL DRESS (1828)
For description, see page 82

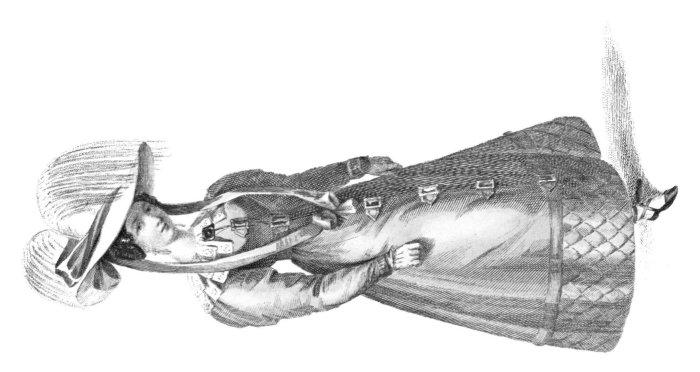

PROMENADE DRESS (1828)
For description, see page 82

WALKING DRESS (1820)

The *pelisse* is composed of *gros de Naples*, of a singular but very beautiful colour, something between a lilac and a purple; it is *wadded*, and the skirt is made pretty full. The waist is ornamented at the bottom by a knot of ribbon. The *pelerine* is of the same material as the pelisse; it is rounded behind, comes only to the point of the shoulder, and tapers down in front. The sleeve is finished at the wrist with a very full trimming of gros de Naples to correspond. The half sleeves and the trimmings round the bottom and up the fronts as well as that which encircles the pelerine are of the same material. Headdress, a bonnet composed of the same material as the pelisse, and lined with white satin. The crown is ornamented with a full bouquet of flowers made of feathers. *Limeric* gloves, and boots the colour of the pelisse.

MORNING DRESS (1821)

A wrapping dress composed of *cashemire*. The body comes up to the throat in the back of the neck, but is a little sloped in front, and turns over all round so as to form a *pelerine*. It wraps across before, and displays a little of the *fichu* worn underneath. The sleeve is easy, but not wide; it is finished at the wrist by folds of *gros de Naples*, to correspond in colour with the dress. The girdle is also of gros de Naples, and fastens with a gold clasp at the side. The skirt wraps across to the left side, and is fastened up the front with bows to correspond. Headdress, a *cornette* composed of full bands of net inserted between plain ones of *letting-in lace*; the ears are cut very narrow, and far back; and it fastens with a full bow of pale pink ribbon under the chin. Black kid shoes.

EVENING DRESS (1820)

A white *gros de Naples round dress*, ornamented at the bottom of the skirt by a broad band of bias white satin disposed in deep *plaits*. This is surmounted by three white satin *rouleaux*, which are wreathed with pearl. The *corsage* is cut low round the bust; it fastens behind, and the back is full. The bust is ornamented with a fulness of white satin, and intermixed with pearls. The shape of the front is formed by a white satin *stomacher* crossed with bands of gros de Naples wreathed with pearl; a pearl button is placed in the middle of each band, and it terminates with a double scallop at the bottom of the waist. A broad white satin sash is disposed in folds round the waist, and tied in a bow and long ends behind. The sleeve is a mixture of white satin and gros de Naples. Hair dressed in light loose ringlets, and much divided on the forehead; the hind hair dressed low. Headdress, a full garland of damask roses, placed rather far back on the crown of the head. White satin shoes, and white kid gloves.

WALKING DRESS (1821)

A *cambric* muslin *round dress*; the bottom of the skirt is trimmed with a flounce of scalloped work, disposed in deep *plaits* at some distance from each other, and the spaces between left plain; in the middle of each space is a muslin tab. This trimming is surmounted by another composed of full puffings of muslin, with lozenges between, and a *rouleau* of muslin at the top. *Spencer* of cerulean blue *soie de Londres*: it is tight to the shape. The waist is finished with a full bow and ends of the same material, corded with satin in the middle of the back. The bust is formed by a fold of satin edged with a loop trimming of soie de Londres, which goes in a sloping direction from the shoulder to the bottom of the waist. The long sleeve is finished at the hand with satin folds and loop trimming: the epaulette is a mixture of satin and soie de Londres. Falling collar, finished with bands of satin and loop-trimming. Headdress, a bonnet composed of white watered *gros de Naples*; the brim turns up a little, and is ornamented under the edge with a band of blue tufted gauze. A piece of gros de Naples goes round the crown, cut at top and bottom in the form of leaves, and edged with narrow straw plait. A bunch of these leaves and a bouquet of marguerites are placed on one side of the crown and a bouquet of marguerites only on the other. White satin ties in a full bow on left side. Black kid shoes.

30

HEADDRESSES (1821)

1. A bonnet composed of *black du cape*: it has a low crown and a very large brim, which is lined with pink *zephyrine*; the edge of the brim is ornamented with a wreath of black satin, disposed in scalloped folds. A full plume of black *marobouts* is placed at the right side of the crown, and a bow of the same material as the bonnet is attached to the base of the plume. Black *gros de Naples* strings.

2. A *ponceau* velvet bonnet lined with white satin. The brim is edged with a *rouleau* of ponceau satin. The velvet is laid in full folds on the crown, which is of an oval shape. A small piece of velvet falls into the neck; a bow of the same material is placed in the centre of the crown, and a wreath of full-blown roses goes round the bottom of it. Ponceau strings.

3. A white satin hat; the crown is low; the brim is small, turns up, and is square on the left side, and rounded, and much deeper on the right side, where a knot of white satin is placed just under the edge. A plume of white flat ostrich feathers, at the base of which is a full bow of white satin, is attached to the right side of the crown.

4. A hat composed of white figured satin; the crown is low. The brim turns up in front; it is shallow at the sides, but deep over the forehead. A plume of white flat ostrich feathers is placed on the right side and droops as low as the left shoulder. This hat is worn over a *cornette* of tulle.

5. A small round cap composed of British net, with a very full border of rich lace; a knot of green ribbon is placed at the right ear, and a similar knot over the forehead, with a bouquet of primroses, surrounded with foliage.

EVENING DRESS (1821)

A low gown made of black *crape* figured with black satin; it is worn over a black *sarsnet* slip. The *corsage* is cut square, and low round the bust, which is decorated with a wreath of white crape leaves, and folds of the same material shade the bosom. The shape of the back is formed in the figure of a heart behind, and finished at the bottom by a full crape bow. Three bands, placed some distance from each other, form the shape at the sides. The trimming of the skirt is composed of plain black crape intermixed with black *gros de Naples*, and silk buttons. The hair is dressed low, and in full but light ringlets at the sides of the face, and very far off the forehead. A wreath of black crape roses goes round the head. Necklace and earrings, jet. Black *chamois* leather shoes and gloves.

COURT DRESS (1821)

A white lace petticoat, of *Urling's* manufacture, over one of white satin. The trimming of the petticoat consists of gold tissue disposed in folds, and edged with gold cord. Train of gold-coloured satin lined with white satin, and trimmed with bunches of gold shells; this trimming goes all round. The *corsage* front is formed of folds, to correspond with the trimming of the petticoat. Sleeves of gold-coloured satin, trimmed with folds of tissue and gold cord; a band of *plaited* cord terminates the sleeve. A very full Elizabeth ruff stands up round the back of the neck. The hair is divided so as to display the forehead very much; it falls in loose ringlets at the sides of the face. The hind hair is dressed low. A diamond *bandeau* is placed very low over the forehead; the *lappets* are of Urling's point lace: a profusion of white ostrich flat feathers finishes the coiffure. Diamond earrings and necklace. White kid gloves, and white satin shoes.

PROMENADE DRESS (1821)

A *pelisse*, composed of dark-violet coloured velvet: the body rather long in the waist and a good deal sloped at each side of the back. The sleeve is terminated by a French cuff. The pelisse wraps across the front, and is trimmed with satin of the same colour. The little bands which separate the heading from the bottom are of velvet, and that trimming goes all round the collar and cuffs, which are trimmed to correspond. A *cashemire* shawl is thrown over the shoulders, and fastened at the throat with a brooch. Lace ruff, made very full. Headdress, a bonnet composed of violet-coloured velvet, and lined with white satin; the shape is very well adapted for walking: it is rather close, but becoming. The brim turns up a little, and is finished just under and above the edge with bands of white *velours natté*. A very full plume of violet-coloured ostrich feathers is placed on one side of the crown. Boots of violet kid. *Limeric* gloves. Ermine muff.

WALKING DRESS (1821)

The *pelisse* is of black *gros de Naples;* the body tight to the shape, and the bust finished in front with black *crape* braiding. The sleeve is adorned at the hand by a broad band of black crape, with a full *rouleau* at each edge. The epaulette consists of large puffs of crape, something in a crescent form, drawn through bands of silk. High standing collar, covered with crape. The bows which fasten the pelisse up the front are also of crape; they are very full, with pointed ends. Headress, a bonnet of black gros de Naples lined with white, and finished at the edge by a double rouleau of black crape; black crape flowers, and gros de Naples strings. The *cornette* worn under the bonnet is of white crape, as is also the ruff. Black *chamois* shoes and gloves.

WALKING DRESS (1822)

The *pelisse* is composed of dove-coloured *lutestring*, lined with rose-coloured *sarsnet*, and *wadded*. The fulness of the skirt is thrown very much behind; a broad band of ermine goes round the bottom, and an extremely novel trimming goes up the fronts. The collar falls over in *pelerine* style; the long sleeve is finished with ermine. Slashed epaulette, with satin folds drawn across the slashes. Headdress, a bonnet of a new cottage shape of rose-coloured lutestring, turned up in front. A bouquet of Provence roses goes all round the crown: rose-coloured strings. Very full lace ruff. Black shoes and *Limeric* gloves.

COURT DRESS (1822)

This elegant robe and petticoat were made for a lady of high rank and taste, as a presentation dress at the Palace of Holyrood. It is of pale blue silver lamé over a blue satin slip; thus combining Scotland's national colours of blue and white, now so prevalent among the leaders of *haut ton* [high style]. The *stomacher* is of silver *vandykes*: a double row extends over the shoulders and back, united by silver roses. The sleeve is short, consisting of a dozen rows of silver vandyke trimming, separated by blue satin pipings. The *tucker* is fine *blond lace*. The robe and petticoat have an elegant border of large roses, of blue *gofre crape* and silver, half encircled with thistles, which form a kind of radii. The trimming is edged with silver wave, and finished with scalloped gofre crape. The headdress is of diamonds, with a superb plume of ostrich feathers. Necklace and earrings of diamonds and sapphires. White kid gloves; white satin shoes, with blue and silver roses.

EVENING DRESS (1822)

The families of the ancient Scotch nobility were distinguished by their different plaids. That represented here is the Mackenzie tartan: it is of very rich silk. The *tucker* is of *crèpe lisse* folded *à la Farinet*, confined in the front, on each side, and on the shoulders by pearl loops. The sleeves short and full, set in a band of twisted satin, and edged with a delicate *Buckinghamshire* lace, ornamented with three circles of rich satin of the same colour as the dress, and united by rose-coloured knots. The band or girdle, *plaited* of various coloured satins, harmonizing with the sleeve and trimming at the bottom of the skirt, which is of two flounces, composed of green net and narrow *rouleaux* of coloured satin, formed like Psyche's wings, and surmounted with a twisted rouleau of satin. Headdress, plaited satin band, with an elegant pearl ornament in the centre: feathers, birds of Paradise. Necklace, earrings, and bracelets of emerald and dead gold. Lilac satin shoes, with green and rose-coloured trimmings. Long white kid gloves. Chinese *crape* fan.

PROMENADE DRESS (1822)

High dress of mulberry-coloured velvet, fastened behind. The collar is unornamented and projecting, and admits a full lace ruff. The long sleeve is finished with a pyramidal ornament of leaves, composed of velvet, edged with a double cord of *gros de Naples*. The epaulette consists of squares of velvet, edged with two rows of *gros de Naples* cord, and fastened at each point with knots of cord. Across the bust, the pyramidal ornament is arranged longitudinally. Broad band of velvet edged with cord round the waist, and fastened behind with an elegant cut steel buckle. At the bottom of the skirt are three rows of chinchilla fur, equidistant. Long *tippet* and muff of chinchilla. Velvet bonnet, to correspond. The front at the edge is trimmed with fluted velvet and interspersed with wolves and teeth, or velvet points, edged with two rows of gros de Naples cord. The crown is low, and a folded *fichu* crosses it in part and ties under the chin. A plume of white ostrich feathers, fastened by a cluster of velvet points, surrounding a steel star, is placed on the right side of the bonnet. Bonnet cap of *blond lace*, with full border. Boots, the same colour as the *pelisse*. Gloves citron colour.

WALKING DRESS (1822)

The *pelisse* is made of silk, of a very delicate pattern, called by the French *peau de papillon* [butterfly skin]; its color is a light shade of marguerite. The body is without any fulness, neat, close, and high. The collar is plain and stands out to admit a large ruff. The upper sleeve is full, and slashed *à l'Espagnole*, confined half way of every division by *ailes de papillon*. Down the front of the pelisse is a plain piece of rich satin, of the same colour, cut bias, and continuing from throat to feet, gradually increasing in width, and on each side ailes de papillon arranged to form chevrons. Bonnet of white *gros de Naples*; the front edged with twisted folds of white and cherry coloured gauze; the flowers are a beautiful Scotch heath with red blossoms, and are intermingled with silk and gauze. Boots, the colour of the pelisse; gloves, lemon colour. The hair is parted, and a few light curls on the temple; the hind hair twisted and fastened on the crown of the head *à l'antique*.

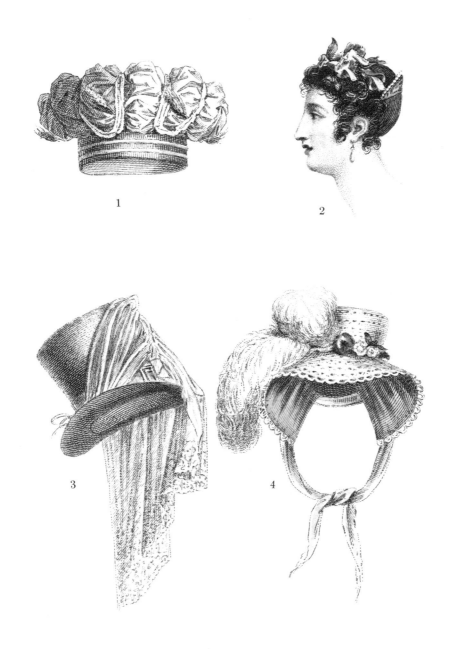

1

2

3

4

HEADDRESSES (1823)

1. Turban of blue *crêpe lisse*, confined with white satin bands edged with *blond lace*, and ornamented with golden ears of corn [wheat].

2. Hair in short full curls on the forehead; ringlets on each side of the ear. A branch of Van Dieman's bells, or *campanule étrangère*, with stamens of spun glass, in front and at the top of the head. The hind hair drawn up plain, and supported by a gold comb.

3. Pale brown beaver riding-hat; a silk band of the same colour and a gold buckle in front. Brussels lace veil.

4. Fancy straw bonnet, lined with rose colour; a plume of white ostrich feathers tipped with rose colour on the right side, and a wreath of anemones and minor convolvuluses round the crown.

PROMENADE DRESS (1824)

Pelisse of *levantine* silk, or Terry velvet, of a rich brown colour (*couleur d'oreille d'ours*), made plain and high to fasten in front, with a neat standing collar, edged with satin of the same colour. The velvet (*velours épingle*) looks like narrow cords. The *ceinture*, which fastens with a gold buckle in front, and the leaves and knots of the trimming, are made of it. The trimming is scalloped, and edged with satin, having a pair of leaflets introduced at each point through a slit, which is bound with satin, and reunited with a velvet knot behind the leaves. The *corsage* is ornamented from the shoulder to the waist, where the trimming approximates, and widens again descend-ing, till it reaches the ermine which goes round the bottom of the pelisse and is a quarter of a yard in depth. The long sleeve has a full epaulette, ornamented with leaves, and the wrist is trimmed to correspond. Bonnet of same material as pelisse, and the inside edged with shaded velvet: the front *à la Marie Stuart*; the round crown is ornamented with velvet flowers and bows of shaded velvet. Bonnet cap of *Honiton*, with very full borders fastening under the chin. Full lace ruff and ruffles. Terry velvet boots, the colour of the pelisse. Pale yellow gloves, and a shell *reticule*, with silver chain.

42

FULL DRESS (1823)

Dress of bright poppy-colour India muslin, ornamented with small sprigs of gold. The *corsage* to fit, with an elegant *stomacher*, composed of double rows of gold lace, placed diagonally from the front and continued over the shoulder; the outside formed into *vandykes*. Short full sleeve, incased in bands edged with gold. Broad gold lace band round the waist. *Tucker* of narrow *blond*. The skirt is decorated with gold lace, placed on the dress in perpendicular double columns of different height; the upper part finished with a wave, and the highest points ter-

minated with three unilateral leaves edged with very narrow blond. Broad *wadded* hem at the bottom of the dress. Turban of gold and poppy-colour *crêpe lisse*; the frame of alternate rows of the same coloured satins brought to a point in front, and satin bands of French folds supporting the large bouffants of crêpe lisse. Short *coquelicot* feather placed on the right side. Pearl earrings, bracelets, and necklace; blond lace scarf; French trimmed gloves, and white satin shoes.

MORNING DRESS (1824)

Shaded striped silk dress of *gros de Naples*; the *corsage à la blouse*; the fulness confined at the top with three satin *rouleaux*, equidistant. Long easy sleeve, finished at the wrist with *rouleaux* of purple and aurora, or orange colour; the upper sleeve very full, and intersected with satin rouleaux, as at the wrist. The skirt touches the ground behind, and is finished with two satin rouleaux, of the darkest shades of each colour. Above is an ornamented crescent, composed of three semicircular bands; the points or horns united by a satin star. Elizabethan ruff of very fine tulle, worked muslin ruffles. *Cornette* or cottage cap of tulle. Border of double tulle, disposed in *bouffants* by alternate rouleaux of aurora and purple satin; one side has a double row of bouffants and a *quilling* of tulle behind. The strings are of broad figured gauze ribbon, cross under the chin, and tie at the top in front of the cap. The hair parted in front, with a few ringlets on each side. Green *cashemire* shawl, and green kid shoes.

44

MORNING DRESS (1824)

Shaded yellow *jaconet* muslin dress; the stripes in waves, with small sprigs of gold colour. The *corsage en blouse*, and the long sleeves *en bouffants*, having seven divisions formed by corded bands, equidistant. Plain cuff, the size of the hand, with a neat worked muslin ruffle. Corded band round the waist, with a plain gold buckle in front. The skirt is neatly trimmed with five double tucks, cut bias, and corded at the top and bottom. Worked muslin square collar, fastened in front with a small buckle. Round cap of white *crêpe lisse*, drawn with amber-colour ribbon, and a large square lace veil. Wrought gold drop earrings. Yellow kid gloves and shoes.

DINNER DRESS (1824)

Dress of pale blue twilled *sarsnet*; the *corsage* cut bias. The front simply ornamented with four satin bands, forming a *stomacher*, and a satin band and *tucker* of fine *blond* round the bust. The sleeve is short and full, arranged in festoons by four satin buttons. A little above the satin band that goes round the arm, on the shoulder, is a full-blown satin rose, with palmated satin leaves pending half way down the sleeve. Broad satin band round the waist, with a rose and palmated leaves pendant behind. The skirt has an elegant satin border of roses surmounted with leaves, arranged in the form of the lotus, and united by festoons. Beneath is a broad satin *rouleau*. White *crêpe lisse* dress hat, ornamented with a garland of damask roses and two long white ostrich feathers, placed on the right side. Richly embroidered scalloped scarf of *Urling's lace*. Necklace and earrings of turquoise. Long white gloves; white satin shoes.

BALL DRESS (1824)

Dress of jonquil-colour silk *barège*, fancifully ornamented with satin bows of the same colour. The *corsage* made rather high; the *stomacher* of jonquil-colour satin, corded all round, and lace in front. It extends across the top of the bust, and ends nearly in a point at the waist, having bows arranged all round at equal distance. On the shoulder is a double row of satin puffing corded at the edges; satin *ceinture*, with triangular leaves formed into a rosette behind. The sleeve is decorated with satin bows, besides a net-work of satin with ornamented knots at each corner. It spreads over the top of the sleeve, and tapers almost to a point, where it unites with the double satin band that goes round the arm. The skirt has two rows of silk barège about half a quarter deep set on very full, and alternately ornamented with satin bows and a broad satin *rouleau* beneath. Turban of white *crêpe lisse*, surmounting a broad band of gold net, richly ornamented with stars at each point, and two gold tassels pendant on left side. Brilliant necklace of sapphire and diamonds; bracelets and earrings to correspond. White kid gloves; white satin shoes. French silk scarf of cerulean blue, with embroidered lace ends.

EVENING DRESS (1825)

Plain colour velvet dress: the *corsage* plain across the bust, and drawn to the shape with a little fulness at the waist; high in front, and falling rather lower on the shoulders, and finished with gold embroidered lace round the top: the sleeves are short with epaulettes formed of heart-shaped leaves, trimmed with *blond lace*. Attached are long full sleeves of white gauze, regulated in front by ribbon velvet passing from under the arm to the lower part of the sleeve, which is confined by three velvet bands round the arm, each fastened by a bow and gold clasp. Blond lace ruffle at the wrist. At the bottom of the skirt is a broad band of satin of the same colour, with small silk cord laid across, forming squares. Gold embroidered *ceinture*, fastened in front with an antique gem. African turban of lilac *barège*, richly embroidered in gold with a band of gold round the head, and supporting the folds over the right ear. The hair parted from the forehead, and three or four large curls on each side. Necklace of medallions in enamel, united by triple chains of gold. Earrings to correspond. English *Thibet* square shawl with embroidered corners. Short white kid gloves; white satin shoes.

EVENING DRESS (1824)

Gold-colour striped gossamer dress: the *corsage* cut straight, and rather high; the upper part full, and ornamented with narrow gold-colour satin *rouleaux*. A trimming of *bouffants*, separated by turban folds, rises from the waist and forms a *stomacher* front; it extends over the shoulder, and meets behind. The sleeve is short and full, and has a row of satin leaves emanating from the band, and spreading half way: the point of each leaf is fastened to a small corded satin band, and attached to the shoulder. Two rows of very full *bouffants*, fastened to the dress by gold-colour satin turban folds, ornament the bottom of the skirt. Dress hat of *crêpe lisse*; the brim circular, with one puffing above and another beneath the edge. Round crown, ornamented with shaded satin ribbon and ostrich feathers of white and amber colour. Necklace, earrings, and bracelets of topaz and turquoise. The earrings large, and of the Chinese bell-shape. French trimmed white kid gloves and white satin shoes.

MORNING DRESS (1824)

Demi-blouse dress of rainbow-shaded *gros de Naples*; the waist long, and the *corsage* full and straight. The sleeves are of the *gigot de mouton* shape; the upper part being very large, and small towards the wrist, where a fulness is introduced and arranged by three flat bands, neatly corded with satin edges. At the bottom of the skirt are four wadded *rouleaux* of the same material as the dress, headed with narrow satin rouleaux and a broad *wadded* hem beneath. Lace or worked muslin frills, *pelerines*, or *collerettes* are usually worn with high silk dresses: this in the print is a richly worked *vandyke* muslin pelerine with ends crossing and confined by a *ceinture* of gros de Naples edged with corded satin. Pale yellow gloves and shoes. *Reticule* of *ponceau* velvet with gold chain and ornaments.

CHILD'S DRESS

A short German frock-coat of superfine bottle-green cloth, with three rows of gilt buttons in front, and braided round the bottom of the skirt with a little tasteful ornament on each side. *Nankeen* vest, trowsers trimmed at the ankles. Worked Spanish collar, or fluted cambric frill.

MORNING DRESS (1824)

Dress of fawn-color *Thibet cloth* or English twilled *cashemire*. The *corsage*, epaulette, and sleeve, are all *à la blouse*; the cuff finished with three bands, and worked muslin ruffles. The skirt has five cross or bias tucks, the same width as the *ceinture*, which fastens behind with a plain gold buckle. *Collerette* of richly worked deep *vandykes*, tied in front with a cord and tassels. The hair *en grandes bouches*. French bonnet of *gros de Naples* of the same colour as the dress; circular broad front, with a small *rouleau* of shaded terry velvet, or *velours épingle*, let in near the edge of the brim and high round the crown which is trimmed to correspond, arranged in puffs behind. In the front is a fan-like trimming of gros de Naples, cut bias, with shaded terry velvet near the edge; the choicest flowers of the winter season are disposed between, as the scarlet fuchsia, the sweet-scented everlasting, and the China rose. Plain gold eardrops. Embroidered blue silk shawl, and fawn-colour morocco shoes.

EVENING DRESS (1825)

Dress of *Urling's lace*, with *Brussels sprigs*: the *corsage* full, circular round the bust, and trimmed with a falling lace. The fulness of the skirt is not entirely set in the band at the back, but slightly introduced in the front and sides. Half way of the skirt is a row of flowers in separate clusters, and beneath are two deep flounces of rich lace, separated by a simple wreath of leaves. The edge of the skirt is scalloped, and a richly embroidered dwarf cistus fills up each space. Blue satin sash, with an embossed gold buckle on right side. Blue satin slip. Turban of blue satin; the bands composed of four longitudinal folds, and a row of French pearls at the edge. The satin full and double round the crown, and two long white ostrich feathers falling backwards. Necklace of pearl, fastened in front with a gold clasp, ornamented with rubies and pearls. Earrings and bracelets to correspond. White kid gloves; white satin shoes.

BALL DRESS (1825)

Dress of pale pink gauze, or *crêpe lisse*, over a white slip: the *corsage à la soubrette*, being made to the shape, and laced with pink cord in the front and back, with an angular drapery edged with white satin. The *corsage* is straight across the bust, and very low on the shoulders. The waist is finished with straps bound with pink satin. The sleeve is extremely short and full, and supported with six shaded pink satin *rouleaux*, formed into a loop and ring, the latter half concealed in the *bouillonnée* of the sleeve. The bottom of the dress is trimmed to correspond, has a very full and deep bouillonnée, surmounted by full-blown pale China roses united by green leaves; from each rose a shaded pink satin rouleau extends over the bouillonnée, and is fastened through the rings which rest on the *wadded* hem beneath. The hair is parted on the forehead and in large curls, intermixed with bows or *noeuds* of pink and hair-colour crêpe lisse; with primroses and poppy-anemones. Necklace of emeralds, with a brilliant star, or Croix de St. Louis, in front; earrings and bracelets to correspond. Long white kid gloves; white satin shoes; circular ivory fan.

DINNER DRESS (1825)

Canary-yellow *gros de Naples*: the *corsage* bias, trimmed at the top of the bust with two rows of ribbon of the same colour, put on very full and fluted. Short sleeve, moderately full, beneath a white *crêpe lisse* full long sleeve, confined at the wrist with a broad gold bracelet, with embossed gold snaps, and a row of turquois above. The dress is decorated with ornamented silk cords, which approximate at the waist, and extend as they descend the corsage or descend the skirt. Each cord is inserted into a double circlet, which unites the points of a row of deep festoons, formed of fluted ribbon corresponding with the trimming of the bust. A broad *rouleau* surrounds the edge of the dress which just touches the ground: broad satin sash of canary-yellow. Silk dress hat, with a gold ornament in front, and a full plume of white ostrich feathers; one is placed beneath the brim, and falls low on the right side of the face. Necklace and earrings of different coloured gems set in gold; gold chain and eye-glass. White kid gloves; white satin shoes.

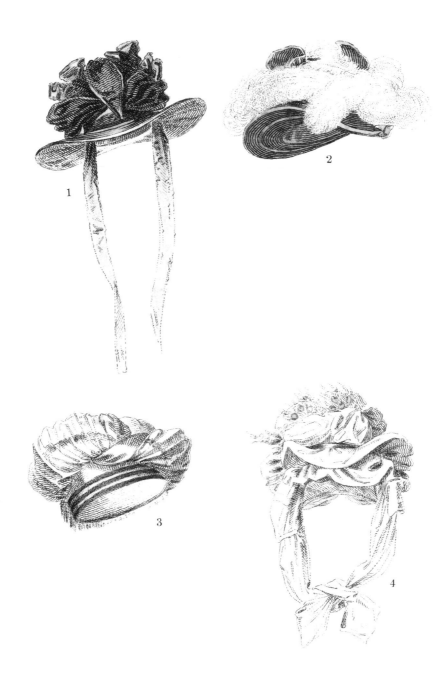

HEADDRESSES (1825)

1. Bonnet of royal purple terry velvet or *velours épingle*; the brim has a corded satin edge; the crown high and rounded at the top, and partially covered with a *fichu* of velvet, bound in satin and ornamented with a small twisted silk cord of the same colour. The trimmings in front are large; the center one is long and narrow, concealing the termination of those on each side. Bows of pearl-edge satin ribbon are disposed about the crown; long strings of the same inside the brim.

2. Black velvet dress hat, bound with gold lace. From a small bow in front, the brim forms double, and small white *marabouts* are introduced between; it is closed behind in a similar manner. Broad gold band round the crown, and at the top four curved ornaments, bound also with gold lace. Marabouts in front and on right side.

3. *Tartarian* turban, formed of a richly shaded striped silk kerchief.

4. Cap of pink and white *crêpe lisse*, with double border and broad strings of same. The crown is high; the back part of white crêpe lisse, full, and arranged by five flat pink satin bands placed perpendicularly, and inserted in the pink satin band at the bottom of the *coul*. The front is formed by *bouffants* of alternate pink and white crêpe lisse, interspersed with pink satin ornaments of a papilionaceous shape, with a profusion of winter cherries or alkakengi, and rosebuds above.

MORNING DRESS (1825)

Dress of fine *jaconet* muslin, ornamented with rose-colour satin ribbon and clear *book muslin*. The *corsage* has three small rows of puffed book muslin round the top, rose-colour satin being drawn through center row, and tied behind. On each side of the bust is a very full piece of book muslin drawn at four equal distances with rose-colour satin, of which a loop or bell is formed on the outside of each drawing. Long sleeve with three drawings towards the wrist; at the shoulder four deep *vandykes* of book muslin made very full, and drawn with rose-colour satin on the outside, each point fastened to the sleeve by a rose-colour bow. The border of the skirt is composed of very full book muslin, with perpendicular drawings of rose-colour satin, terminating with a bow at the top. Cape or *pelerine* of the same material as the dress is fastened with an oval amethyst brooch, and trimmed round with two *rouleaux* of puffed book muslin, rose-colour satin being drawn through one. *Chip* hat, trimmed flowers; rose-colour *crêpe lisse* gauze veil. Lemon-colour gloves, and morocco shoes.

CHILD'S DRESS

Dark green Highland plaid dress: rose-colour tartan stockings; Highland cap and feathers.

MORNING DRESS (1825)

Dress of lavender-colour *gros de Naples*: the *corsage* made rather high and shaped at the back; the fulness regulated at the top by three narrow bands, or silk braid of the same colour. The sleeve is confined at the wrist with three ornaments of different lengths, narrowing towards the cuff. The skirt is trimmed with four notched rows of the same material as the dress, two rows pointing upwards, and the others falling downwards, and a fluted band, encircled with a *rouleau*, adorns the centre; beneath is a *wadded* hem. Epaulette braces, of pink and white gros de Naples, meet in a point behind, extend in a slanting direction to the shoulders, cross in front, with long ends loose from the *ceinture*, which is the same as the dress. The epaulette is trimmed with a double row of pink and white quilted ribbon. The cap is made to correspond, being formed of pink and white and lilac gros de Naples, and a border of Grecian lace. Two rouleaux extend across the crown, composed of the three different colours; the hindermost has a bow of pink ribbon attached, the same as the strings. Lilac kid shoes.

EVENING DRESS (1825)

Dress of pink *gros de Naples*: the *corsage* has a slight fulness in front with a thin drapery of folded gauze of the same colour, beginning at the shoulder, with a pink satin star composed of four leaves, each leaf having one deep notch, and a knot or button in the centre of the star uniting the points of the leaves. The sleeve has five divisions, each formed by two satin notched leaves, united by a button, and placed perpendicularly round sleeve. The skirt has a rich border of *crêpe lisse bouffant* with pairs of notched leaves, arranged to correspond with the sleeves. A broad satin *rouleau* heads the trimming, and at the bottom is a *wadded* hem. Above is a row of crêpe lisse puffs, placed obliquely, and fastened at the top with a small satin button, and finished at the opposite end with three pink satin notched leaves, united by a button. Broad satin sash, with gold buckle on the left side, and two small bows; the ends long and fringed. White crêpe lisse *tucker*, and long full sleeves, confined by broad gold bracelets. The hair is dressed in large curls. Gold earrings and gold chain and eye-glass. White satin shoes, and short white kid gloves.

58

HEADDRESSES (1825)

TOP. Fine British *Leghorn* hat; brim large, flat; the crown moderately high; round it a lilac satin ribbon with a bow on the left side, from it rises a fanciful trimming in lilac *gros de Naples*, edged with straw-colour satin. Another trimming is introduced midway, and rising circularly, finishes with a small bouquet of fancy flowers on the left side. A bouquet is also placed on the right side, but higher. Strings of lilac satin, and a bow on the right, inside brim.

CENTER, LEFT. Turban of scarlet or pomegranate-colour *crêpe lisse*, with large close longitudinal folds, confined in front by a broad gold band placed obliquely. The head-piece of gros de Naples, pointed in front, and edged with gold lace.

CENTER, RIGHT. Cap of white crêpe lisse: the crown is circular, and formed by two rows of large puffs, edged with pink satin, having a wreath of China roses beneath the upper row, and round the headpiece, within each puff, a sprig of arbutus and geranium. The border is very full and deep, and ties under the chin with pink satin ribbon.

BOTTOM. Pale blue dress hat, fluted, and the brim edged with narrow *blond lace*; the crown surrounded by a wreath of blue satin leaves, tied in pairs by a satin knot, each leaf deeply notched. White ostrich feathers are arranged round the crown, the highest being in the front.

59

PROMENADE DRESS (1825)

Wadded pelisse of *gros de Naples* of a bright geranium colour, lined with white *sarsnet*: the *corsage* made to shape, with a square standing collar, edged with satin, and fastened in front with two gold buttons; broad *ceinture* with satin corded edges, fastened in the same manner. Long, full sleeve confined between the shoulder and the elbow with a band and button, and five bands equidistant from the wrist towards the elbow. The front of the pelisse is ornamented with three bias tucks on each side, which meet at the waist, and increase in breadth and distance as they reach the shoulder, or descend to the bottom of the skirt, where they turn off circularly, and are continued round to the opposite side, where they unite with the tucks in front, and interlacing with them form a festoon on each side. Beneath is a broad wadded hem. Pamela hat of royal purple velvet, edged with a small *rouleau* of satin. The hat is trimmed with shaded gold-coloured ribbon round the crown, and five bows and long ends, fringed on the right side. Broad strings of the same withinside. Cottage cap of sprigged net, a full narrow border of British lace. Narrow frill and ruffles of the same. Long drop gold earrings and embossed gold chain twice around the throat. Dark sable muff. Yellow kid gloves and shoes.

PROMENADE DRESS (1825)

Pelisse of lilac *gros de Naples*; the collar stiffened, and turned half over. The *corsage* is made full longitudinally, and confined by a band and a row of lilac silk buttons down the center of the front and back. The shoulders also have a band, but without buttons. The sleeves are *en gigot*, finished with bands at the wrist. The *ceinture* is rather broad, and ornamented behind by two silk frogs of the same colour as the pelisse; a *rouleau* of the same breadth as the hem, and sep- arated by a space of equal width, which surrounds the bottom of the skirt. *Cornette* of tulle, with a narrow full border. Bonnet of British *Leghorn*, very fine and light, and trimmed with double white *crêpe lisse* edged with blue satin, beginning at the bottom of the crown in front, and rising across to the top at the back, where it is formed into a bow. Brussels lace veil. Strawberry-colour shoes and gloves. Green parasol lined with a pale rose-colour *sarsnet*.

61

MORNING DRESS (1825)

Pelisse of Pomona or apple-green *gros de Naples*, fastened in front with circular silk buttons of the same colour. A single *rouleau,* about an inch and a half broad, surrounds the edge of the skirt just above the *wadded* hem. The sleeve is *en gigot* and slit at the wrist, and buttons; the band of waist is corded, and buttons. The *pelerine* or cape is composed of alternate rows of gros de Naples or ribbon, the colour of the pelisse, and of myrtle green. It is notched or *vandyked* the breadth of each division. Square embroidered *collerette* of French cambric. Hat formed, like the pelerine of two shades of green; a bouquet of hyacinth or haw-bells and blossoms of the mezerion on the left side; gold earrings, and bracelets outside the sleeve; chain and eye-glass. Pale yellow shoes; bronze-colour parasol and shoes.

EVENING DRESS (1826)

Dress of geranium-colour *gros de Naples*: the *corsage* is trimmed around the top with a notched *ruche* of the same material. A light folded drapery, in the form of a *stomacher*, adorns the bust. The sleeve is short and extremely full, and set in a satin corded band, with long white *crêpe lisse* sleeves, inserted at the shoulder and confined at the wrist with broad bead bracelets and ornamented *mancherons*. The skirt is made to wrap, and is shaped circularly on the right, just above the *wadded* hem of the petticoat (which is of the same gros de Naples as the dress), and is trimmed with two double ruches, deeply notched made of Italian patent *crape* (manufactured by Noailles, a manufactury at Greatness, Kent). The *ceinture* is of gros de Naples, edged with corded satin of the same colour, and supporting a gold watch set with rubies, and gold chain and trinkets. The hair is in large curls, and forms a kind of antique wreath round the head. A cluster of winter-flowers is placed on the right side. Earrings of pearl and gold; shaded gauze scarf; white satin shoes.

PROMENADE DRESS (1826)

Pelisse of satin *Turque*, or Turkish satin, of a rich myrtle-green, *wadded*, and lined with rose-coloured *sarsnet*. The *corsage* made the straight way, and full both in the back and front, and set in gathers in the band, and is ornamented from the throat to the feet with large mother-of-pearl buttons. Double *pelerine* or cape deeply *vandyked*, and edged with very narrow chinchilla fur, to correspond with the muff and broad chinchilla fur at the bottom of the skirt. Buttons and trimmings (when not of fur) are generally of the same material as the pelisse. Black velvet hat, bent in front; the crown ornamented with a profusion of velvet bows, and a gold slider in the centre. Rose-colour strings, the same as the ribbon round the throat, which ties in two bows and long ends, supporting the *collerette* of worked muslin. The hair in ringlets; and a cap *à trois pièces*, with a narrow full border, fastened under the chin. High walking shoes of black leather, lined and edged with fur.

DINNER DRESS (1826)

Turkish satin dress of lemon-colour, closed in front, and ornamented with buttons of the same material, placed very near each other. A *rouleau, en serpent,* fastened by a circlet in the front just above the *ceinture,* rises to the shoulder, where another circlet confines it, and passing over, ornaments the back in a similar manner. The sleeve is decorated with five trimmings formed of double *plaits,* regulated by a rouleau in the centre. The skirt has a light border composed of two rouleaux, placed in a waving direction; and from a circlet that encompasses the lower part of the wave, proceeds an ornament corresponding to those on the sleeve. The rouleau in the centre is terminated by a button, and arranged semicircularly, beneath is a broad *wadded* hem. The sash is long, and of the same colour as the dress, but richly adorned with shaded leaves of deeper hue, and fastened on the right side with a highly wrought gold buckle. White satin hat, edged with chenille, turned up in front, and confined by a loop of citron-colour Italian *crape,* fastened by a pearl ornament with a large ruby in the centre; bird of Paradise on the right side and bows of citron-colour Italian crape. Pearl necklace, fastened by a ruby clasp; medallion bracelets, outside the long gloves, shoes of the same material as dress.

BALL DRESS (1826)

Dress of fine tulle over a white satin slip; the *corsage* is bound with white satin, from which falls a deep blond scalloped lace, doubled on the shoulders, and forming a kind of epaulette to the short sleeve which is finished with a narrower scalloped blond lace. A Provins rose is placed on the left side of the bust, and a satin corkscrew trimming in the form of a *stomacher* regulates the fulness of the corsage. The skirt is ornamented with two rows of festoons, edged with three narrow pipings of cherry-coloured satin, the centre of the upper festoon being attached to the points of the lower by a full-blown Provins rose, suspended by a narrow white satin corkscrew trimming. In the lower festoon the roses are attached to the broad white satin *rouleau* at the bottom of the dress. A bouquet of Provins roses and Eastern hyacinths is placed at the termination of each festoon of the upper row. Broad satin sash of cherry-colour, tied on the left side. The hair is divided in the Madonna style, and ornamented with a wreath of French pearl beads and full-blown Provins roses, brought from behind the right ear to

the front and entwining a bow of hair on the crown of the head. *Blond* spotted scarf; long white kid gloves, with bracelets outside. Necklace and earrings of white cornelian and embossed gold; white satin shoes.

YOUNG LADY'S DRESS

Frock of white *crêpe lisse*; the corsage full and edged with ethereal blue satin, and a narrow trimming of *blond* lace beneath. The skirt is ornamented with four pipings of blue satin; three rise circularly half way up the left side, and are terminated with blue satin bows. Blue satin slip; white cambric trowsers, finished with delicately scalloped work, and ornamented with two pipings of blue satin; broad blue satin sash tied behind. The hair parted in front, and in ringlets *à la Vandyke*. Pearl necklace, gold chain, and a cornelian heart. Gold bracelets outside the long white kid gloves; white silk stockings; blue satin shoes, with sandals.

66

WALKING DRESS (1826)

Pelisse of straw-coloured *gros de Naples*, fastened in front. The collar low, and projecting as it reaches the back, admitting a narrow *ruche* of fine tulle. The waist is long and drawn behind. The sleeves, large and full to the elbow, are finished with a plain neat cuff. The skirt is trimmed down the front with the same material by a continuation of scrolls, enlarging as they descend, attached on the outside by buttons, and within united by their circular terminaton. *Pelerine* or *fichu* of straw-coloured gros de Naples like the pelisse, trimmed with a double ruche, narrow at the *ceinture*, and expanding towards the shoulders. Hat of straw-colour gros de Naples; the brim large, circular, and flat in front, but shallow behind, ornamented with rays of royal purple ribbon, and a bow at the edge on the left side. The strings uncut; the crown rather high, fully and fancifully trimmed on the right side with broad purple and straw-colour ribbon. *Cornette* of tulle; the hair in large curls; red cornelian brooch, earrings, and bracelets. Gloves of pale blue kid; geranium-colour shoes; pale rose-colour parasol, with a white border.

BALL DRESS (1826)

Crêpe-lisse dress of Haytian blue: the *corsage* has a narrow notched *tucker* and *Farinet* folds of white crêpe lisse across the bust, and a small bouquet of spring flowers in front. The sleeves are ornamented with two notched *ruches* of white crêpe lisse, and a narrow blue satin *rouleau*. The lower extending all round the arm, midway of the sleeve; and other only across the top. The skirt is ornamented with a row of Persian roses, attached by bows of blue satin ribbon, two of the ends extending to a handsome wreath of *folia peltata* in blue satin. A row of puffed crêpe lisse, and a narrow satin *wadded* hem terminate the bottom of the dress. Blue satin sash, with short bows and long ends, fastened on the left side. Headdress of three folds of Haytian blue crêpe lisse, with four rows of pearl beneath, placed between large bows of hair, and *plaits* arranged in festoons on the left side, and one single bow on the right, drawn very tight and fastened by a comb. Necklace, earrings, and bracelets of gold, ruby and pearls; long white kid gloves; white satin shoes.

DINNER DRESS (1826)

Dress of Pomona green *gros de Naples*: the *corsage* is ornamented with folds of shaded *grenadine*, which diverge from a cameo in the centre of the *crêpe lisse tucker*, pass across the bust and meet in a bow behind. The sleeves are short and rather full, with sleeves *en gigot* in white crêpe lisse over them, which are confined at the wrist with tartan bead bracelets fastened by a cameo. The skirt has two rows of fluted lozenges in shaded grenadine; the longitudinal points connected by a broad flat band of gold-coloured grenadine. Beneath is a broad *wadded* hem or *rouleau*. The headdress is very large, and composed of shaded *barège* or grenadine, with a profusion of white ostrich feathers on the left side. The hair parted in front and arranged in large curls. Gold earrings *à la Flamande;* gold chain and necklace. Circular *reticule* of *ponceau* velvet, edged with gold, and trimmed with British lace; strings of ponceau and white satin. Short white gloves; white satin shoes; painted gauze fan.

69

MORNING DRESS (1826)

Dress of sea-green *gros de Naples*; the *corsage* is ornamented with nine-corded bands, placed longitudinally and equidistant at the sides, but formed into three separate divisions in front, each uniting three bands and confined with a button. The sleeves are large and full to the elbow and are terminated in a corded band; the fulness is regulated by a broad band which extends from the shoulder downwards. The skirt is decorated with bows and festoons of ribbon of the same colour, support-ing Italian *crape* baskets; broad *wadded* hem beneath. Fluted muslin *collerette*, shallow in front, but widening as it proceeds towards the shoulder, and fastened by a cameo. Gold chain and eyeglass. The hair arranged in large curls, and a gold comb confining a long bow of hair on the top of the head; gold earrings and bracelets; shaded ribbon *reticule*, of a similar shape to the baskets that ornament the dress; yellow gloves and shoes.

70

EVENING DRESS (1826)

White *crêpe lisse* worn over a white satin slip. The *corsage* full, and ornamented with a rose-colour satin cape, corded at the edge, very narrow at its conjunction in front, and extending like zephyr's wing as it reaches the shoulder, where two ornamented scallops unite it with a similar wing or cape behind. The short under-sleeve has a long full sleeve over it terminated at the wrist with a white satin *Vandyke* cuff, and fastened by a broad gold bracelet with a medallion clasp. The skirt has a deep border of rose-colour satin arranged in two rows; the upper ornament is salver-shaped supporting an oval composed of flat bands like trellis work. Beneath are two broad rose-colour *rou-*leaux. The headdress is a kind of turban, formed of rose-colour bands, interwoven like trellis work; the crown is long and rather small towards the top, very similar in shape to the *Likanian* cap. A white crêpe lisse rouleau, in *bouffants* entwined by rose-colour bands, reaches round it, lessening as it approaches the right side where an ornament in rose-colour satin, doubled and in large *plaits*, extends over the ear. The hair in large curls on the left side, and *à la Madonna* on the right; necklace of medallions united by rows of gold beads; earrings *à la Flamande*; shaded gauze scarf, fringed; white kid gloves; white satin shoes.

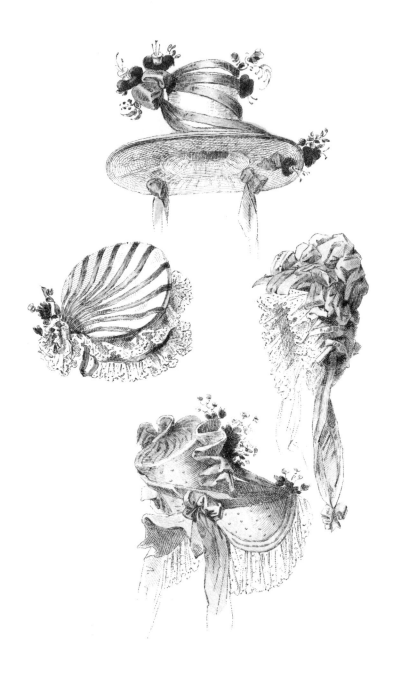

HEADDRESSES (1826)

TOP. Hat of rice-straw; bound with green satin ribbon of the colour of the waters of the Nile; on the outside of the edge, and within the brim on the left side, are small branches of the beautiful Peruvian browalia, from which proceed two ribbons as far as the top of the crown on the right side, where they are interrupted by a cluster of browalias. They descend again and go round the crown, thus crossing four times in front, a smaller branch of browalia is placed on the opposite side. Two bows are attached to les *brides*, or strings withinside the brim.

CENTER, LEFT. Cap of white *crêpe lisse*; the crown *à la biret*, ornamented with blue satin *rouleaux* spreading from the back; the head-piece is trimmed profusely with deep *blond lace*, a Provins rose, and waving crêpe lisse edged with blue satin.

CENTER, RIGHT. French *demi-toilette* cap of lilac gauze; the crown is very full and arranged *en bouffes*. Gold-colour shaded gauze ribbon in front with full trimmings of lilac gauze, bound with shaded gold-colour gauze. Long loose strings of the same with the short end fastened sometimes on the opposite side. Deep full border of British lace.

BOTTOM. Bonnet of sprigged rose-colour *gros de Naples*; the brim is ornamented with two rose-colour satin rouleaux and a curtain *blond lace* veil more than half-a-quarter deep: behind is a stiffened silk trimming; the brim not extending to the back. The crown has a waving trimming and a large cluster of arbutus in front, and also at the edge of the brim, from whence proceeds a rose-colour crêpe lisse to the opposite side of the crown, the top of which is arranged in waving flutes, and at the edge is a shell-like ornament.

PROMENADE DRESS (1827)

High dress of striped *gros de Naples, wadded* and lined with scarlet *sarsnet*. The *corsage* is made up to the throat with a little fulness towards the waist which is confined by a rich plaid scarf, worn as a sash, and tied in front. The border of the skirt is an horizontal fan-like trimming of scarlet *corded point*, and is crossed in the centre by longitudinal green velvet fluted puffs; their terminations united by circlets of scarlet satin and green velvet. Beneath is a row of chinchilla fur. The sleeves are *en gigot*, and stiffened to keep them extended: they are confined at the wrist by a scarlet corded band, fastened with a gold clasp. A *vandyke* cuff extends a little way over the hand, and a second corded band regulates the fulness between the elbow and the wrist. Chinchilla fur adorns the shoulders and surrounds the throat. Bonnet of the same material as the dress; brim edged with a *rouleau*, and lined with scarlet satin. The crown is almost concealed by its decorations, consisting of three hydrangea and several large green velvet leaves, besides bows of gros de Naples, which are placed on the left side. The hair is dressed in a double row of large curls; the earrings are low and of coral; yellow gloves lined with fur; chinchilla muff, and boots of slate-colour morocco.

EVENING DRESS (1827)

Dress of white *crêpe lisse*, over a lavender-colour Turkish satin slip. The *corsage* is full; the sleeves are in the Chinese taste, and are formed of four divisions, with projecting points half-way, edged with lavender-coloured satin, and terminating round the arm with a broad satin band, edged with narrow *blond*. *Tucker* of the same. The skirt is decorated with three rows of the same material as the dress, ornamented with small lavender-colour satin *rouleaux*, *en carreaux*, and large roses of *emarginate* satin leaves, with crêpe lisse centres; beneath is a rouleau of satin. Sicilian gauze scarf; lavender-colour sash tied behind in short bows and long ends. The hair is dressed in large curls, and the headdress composed of a wreath of roses and large bows of lavender-colour Italian *crape*. Embossed gold pagoda earrings, and necklace with a cameo locket. Gold bracelets, with cameo clasps outside the gloves, which are of white kid. White satin shoes.

EVENING DRESS (1827)

Dress of black *gros de Naples*; the *corsage* cut bias and ornamented with a fluted trimming of black Italian *crape*, narrow in front, and gradually deepening to the shoulder. The short sleeve is set in a band; the long sleeve is large, and of crape, with coronet cuff of gros de Naples, fastened by a wrought iron cameo clasp. The skirt is ornamented with an intermixture of gros de Naples and a crape of a fanciful pattern, headed by a narrow *rouleau* of satin, which is repeated between the trimming, and the skirt is terminated by a *wadded* hem. The headdress consists of a very full wreath of black crape flowers, and a light *crêpe lisse* hat, *à la Marie Stuart*, with long *lappets* reaching to the waist. Large diamond-shaped black brooch in the front of the bust. German cast-iron necklace, earrings, and bracelets with cameo clasps. Black kid gloves and *chamois* shoes.

EVENING DRESS (1827)

Turkish satin dress of pale blue; the *corsage* is trimmed round the bust with embroidered *blond lace*, shallow in front but deep and full on the shoulders and back. The short sleeves are composed of perpendicular rows of blond set in a blue satin band round the arm. The skirt has a very deep flounce of scalloped blond lace, headed by an open diamond-shape satin trimming, with a band passing longitudinally through each space, and forming a St. Andrew's cross at every change. Beneath the flounce are narrow *rouleaux* entwined. The headdress is a *toque* of garter-blue satin, with a train band of various coloured stones. Three ostrich feathers are placed in front, and two, falling very low, on each side. The earrings, necklace and bracelets are of filigree gold, with medallions of different coloured stones. Gold chain and eyeglass, watch, chain and trinkets. White kid gloves, trimmed; white satin shoes.

BALL DRESS (1827)

Dress of rose-colour *crêpe lisse* over a white slip; the *corsage* full, and edged with an entwined narrow *rouleau*, beneath a *blonde tucker*. The sleeves are short, and set in a rose-colour satin band, and partly encased by tulip-leaves, forming a kind of calyx. The skirt has three rows of graduated satin leaves, each division forming a cone, the top commencing with a diamond-shaped leaf, then a ring of satin, then tulip-leaves; a small double satin rouleau follows, and heads the next row of tulip-leaves, which are larger than those above and smaller than those beneath. The whole is finished by a large satin rouleau. Rose-colour sash, tied behind. The hair in large curls in front, with ringlets on each side behind the ears. Long white kid gloves, trimmed with a *quilling* of tulle at the top. Gold earrings, bracelets, and necklace, with emerald clasps. Rose-colour embroidered satin shoes.

MORNING DRESS (1827)

Pomegranate-colour *gros de Naples* dress, checked with black and a deeper shade of pomegranate. The body is high and full, and the sleeves *en gigot*. The skirt has a little fulness in front, and is trimmed with three deep bias tucks, the upper not so broad as the two lower. *Vandyked* tulle *pelerine*, with falling circular collar, edged with white satin, and meeting just above the waist. The *vandykes* are progressively large to the shoulder, where they are very deep, and lessen again towards the back. Sprigged lace cap, placed rather forward; the border broad and full, with cross-barred blue gauze ribbon between the spaces in front. Above the border the ribbon is plain as far as the temple, from whence it is pressed round the back part of the cap. The crown is full and regulated by blue ribbon. The hair is dressed in ringlets. Plain gold earrings: eyeglass suspended by a black ribbon formed into a loop, and confined at the throat by a gold filigree slider, ornamented with rubies. Black velvet bracelets and sash, with short bows and pointed ends; blue kid gloves; black shoes of *gros des Indes*.

SEASIDE COSTUME (1827)

Dress of canary-colour *gros de Naples*, with narrow stripes; the *corsage* made full and rather high. The skirt has two deep flounces, of the same material as the dress; the lower set on straight, and very full; the upper in four festoons. The flounces are each headed by a flat band of canary-colour gros de Naples, edged with orange-colour satin *rouleaux*. *Pelerine* of the same, drawn behind, slashed on the shoulders, and extending below the *ceinture* in front which is ornamented by a band, edged on each side with orange-colour satin. *Gigot* sleeves of plain *jaco-*

net muslin, fastened at the wrists with black velvet bracelets. Circular embroidered *collerette* tied with canary-colour ribbon. British *Leghorn* hat; the brim very large and circular, and ornamented within side, near the edge, by a rouleau of lilac *crêpe lisse*, entwined with canary-colour satin ribbon. The crown is decorated with large feather-flowers, puffs of lilac crêpe lisse, and twisted rouleau. Lilac strings tied on the left side. Lilac kid gloves; yellow morocco shoes.

CARRIAGE DRESS (1827)

High dress of green Merino, with *gigot* sleeves and broad wristbands confining the gloves which are of rose-colour kid. The skirt is trimmed with two deep flounces of the same material as the dress, headed and edged with a shawl pattern border of roses. Cloak of tomata-colour *gros de Berlin*, lined with ermine, made very long and full, and drawn at the waist behind. The armholes are bound with tomata-colour velvet, like the circular cape which is fastened in front with a gold clasp *à la militaire*. Square collar, falling over and displaying the ermine lining. Blue silk *Navarino* handkerchief tied round the throat. White *gros de Naples* hat with a wide and spreading brim, ornamented beneath with rows of tomata-colour satin ribbon, on each side united by a ribbon extending across the front. The crown is decorated with white and tomata-colour satin trimming, and white ostrich feathers disposed in front and at the sides. Satin strings *en bride*. Muff of ermine, and shoes of dark chestnut-colour kid.

PROMENADE DRESS (1827)

Pelisse of lavender-colour watered *gros de Naples*. The *corsage* is made rather open at the throat to display a full *chemisette* of French *cambric*, with a square worked *collerette* falling over. The pelisse fastens in front with hooks and eyes, and is decorated with bows. A broad band, edged with satin of the same colour, descends from the waist, goes round and forms the border of the pelisse, and is ornamented by a row of painted leaves, with *rouleau* satin binding, which is continued over the bust and meets behind. The sleeves are *en gigot*, and have broad waistbands, with printed leaves to correspond; *ceinture* edged with satin. Rose-colour hat of watered gros de Naples; the brim extremely large with a blond curtain veil, a quarter of a yard deep, the crown has a trimming in the form of large leaves, with rose-colour satin rouleau binding, and a bouquet of flowers on each side. The strings are of a broad satin ribbon, and descend from a bow on the left side; they are very long and untied, and have each a bow at the end. Gold earrings, chain and cross; yellow gloves; black kid shoes.

81

PROMENADE DRESS (1828)

Pelisse of apple-green *gros de Naples*, closed in front and fastened by gold buckles, with angular straps corded at the edge of the same material as the pelisse. *Gigot* sleeves, with corded indented triangular cuffs, pointing upwards. The skirt is full at the back and sides and a small space left plain in front. The border is of chenille *en treillis*, the corners confined by circlets of apple-green satin; broad corded band above, fastened in front by a gold buckle. *Collerette* of French *cambric*, composed of two rows of pendant straps, embroidered in a satin stitch. Large circular hat, of white *gros de Naples*, edged with rose-colour satin, placed rather forward, and displaying a row of curls behind. A plume of rose-colour quadrille feathers adorns the right side, which fall in opposite directions, the end of one extending over the front and left side of the brim, the other drooping backwards. Round the corner is a broad rose-colour satin ribbon folded diagonally, and terminating in a long bow beneath the feathers. Withinside the brim are two bows from which long lawn strings proceed, ornamented with bows and ends at the extremities. Red cornelian earrings and brooch; gold bracelets with red cornelian clasps; short kid gloves of primrose-colour; black satin Parisian shoes and sandals.

HEADDRESSES (1828)

Top. Hat of *couleur monstre*, or light green striped velvet; the brim, extremely wide, contains behind half a quarter deep and full, being a continuation of the lower velvet trimming that surrounds the crown, placed low on the left and high on the right. Papilionaceous bows of rich satin ribbon, of cherry-colour and black, adorn the left side, and spread from the top of the crown towards the right. Three small branches of the golden or Portuguese everlasting fall from opposite points.

Center, left. *Toque* of fine tulle spreading upwards from a broad gold band, which has two bows and an end pendant from the right side. The toque is edged at the top with gold lace; the crown is low and full, and has a star in the centre.

Center, right. Turban of crimson velvet, with two ostrich feathers of the same colour on the right side, and a projecting ornament of black velvet, bound with gold lace, on the left. *Bandeau* of ermine.

Bottom. Parisian hat of black velvet, bound with gold-colour satin and lined with pink. The brim is very large and double in front; two curled ostrich feathers of scarlet and gold emanate from the space between and one extends beyond the edge of the brim. The crown has a fan-like bow of gold and black satin ribbon, and a large ostrich feather attached to the centre. Strings of gold and black satin ribbon.

BALL DRESS (1828)

Crêpe lisse of bird of Paradise yellow, with short full sleeves set in a black satin band round the arm. *Stomacher* front, composed of five perpendicular divisions widening towards the top of the bust, and displaying black satin puffings between. Scalloped *blond* trimming in front, deepening to a zephyr cape on the shoulders and at the back. The point of the stomacher is low and finished with a *ruche* of tulle. The skirt is short, and ornamented with three rosaceous borders of the same material as the dress, with black satin puffings at the corners, and is terminated with a yellow satin *rouleau*. A band of the same colour is arranged between each of the borders. The hair is dressed in large curls in front, high on the top, and ornamented with tulle drapery, and supported with a tiara comb. Necklace, earrings and bracelets of embossed gold and turquoise; white kid gloves; French trimmed gold tissue shoes and sandals.

BALL DRESS (1828)

White tulle over *à Feodore* blue satin slip. The waist is long, and pointed back and front, and bound with gold lace. The *stomacher* extends to the top of the shoulder, where it terminates in an obtuse angle, projecting over the sleeves, and united to an angular cape. A branch of white Persian roses spreads over the front; stomacher is terminated with a rosaceous ornament of rubies set in gold. The sleeves are short and full, and kept out by the stiffened sleeves of the slip. The skirt is bound with white satin, open in front, but united at regular distances by five rosaceous ruby clasps set in gold. Branches of white Persian roses form the border: it is a quarter yard shorter than the slip, which is terminated by a blue satin *rouleau*. The hair is parted in front, dressed in large bows, and adorned with papilionaceous bows of blue and gold tissue ribbon. White kid gloves; medallion bracelets outside. Earrings *à la Flamande*; gold necklace with a diamond-shape locket in front. Gauze scarf; white satin shoes.

HEADDRESSES (1828)

1. Cap of white *crêpe lisse*, the border very broad, *vandyked* and edged with scarlet braiding. In a deep puff on the left temple a cardinal flower is placed. The border touches the forehead in front, takes a retrograde direction and rises high on the right side, and is sustained with another branch of the cardinal flower. The head-piece is bound with scarlet satin.

2. *Toque* of Parisian gauze of pale Pomona green, folded very deep and standing up from the head-piece, and adorned with several long bows of broad green gauze ribbon. The crown is low and circular.

3. Hat of Aurora or amber-colour *gros de Naples*; the crown higher in front than behind, and the front of the brim very projecting and shallow at the back, where a small bow is placed, to which a long white ostrich feather is fastened. It lies flat on the brim, and falls below it towards the left. A zig-zag puff trimming ornaments the front. Broad amber-colour strings.

4. *Capote* of rose-colour silk, trimmed with a notched ruche at the edge of the brim, and lined with white *sarsnet*. The crown is high, and in front has two very large stiffened bows like long loops and a triplet of leaves standing erect.

CARRIAGE DRESS (1828)

Gros de Naples high dress of Pomona green, ornamented with three deep flounces of the same, each having at the top a border of York and Lancaster rose arranged alternatively. The sleeves are very full, and confined twice above the elbow with rose-colour satin bands, fastened with square gold buckles. Beneath the elbow it is made to fit the arm, and is laced above half way, and has a rose-colour cord and tassel pendant.

Corded rose-colour satin belt, pointed in front, with small bows behind. *Ruche* of tulle, and *pelerine* of the same, scalloped at the back, and reaching to the belt in front. *Leghorn* hat, circular and large, trimmed with rose-colour satin ribbon and artificial flowers; tied under the right ear in a large bow, and full long ends of rose-colour *crêpe lisse*. Primrose-colour gloves and shoes.

GLOSSARY

Names and their meanings, like fashions, change with the times. The definitions in this glossary are meant to explain the terms in the context of the period covered in this book, 1818–28. Some may seem farfetched or excessive, others so obscure as to defy definition today, but this was not unusual for an age so wrapped in romanticism that ordinary language seemed less than adequate and too prosaic for the needs of fashion.

Aërophane crape. A fine, airy, crimped crepe, almost transparent

À Feodore. An obscure term used with reference to satin. Possibly derived from Feodore, an officer of the ancient Court of Wards.

Aigrette. Tuft or plume of feathers.

Ailes de papillon. Cloth ornaments arranged to suggest the wings of a butterfly.

À la biret. In the style of a beret or a biretta.

À la blouse. Wide, ample, full, unconfined.

À la Farinet. Reference of term obscure, probably meaning raised like die-cut surface.

À la Flamande. In the Flemish manner, in this series applying to long, dangling earrings.

À la Madonna. A hairstyle, center-parted and simply arranged, like that of Madonnas in Italian paintings.

À la Marie Stuart. Hats or bonnets dipping to a point in front, a style associated with the headdresses worn by Marie Stuart, Queen of Scots (1542–87).

À la militaire. In the military style.

À la Van Dyke. In the styles recorded in the paintings by Van Dyck (1599–1641).

À l'antique. In the manner of the Greeks of antiquity.

À l'Espagnol. In the Spanish style, referring to the slashes of the 16th century and the fitted bolices of women's costumes of the 16th and 17th centuries.

Athenian braces. Bands of soft folds emulating Greek drapery.

À trois pièces. In three parts.

Bandeau (pl. bandeaux). A narrow band worn either on the head or on the costume for decorative purposes.

Barège. Very fine material, generally of silk and wool, with silk thrown to the surface giving the fabric a silky, foamy texture.

Black du cape. Term obscure, possibly a special fabric used for millinery.

Blond lace. A lace made of fine mesh with patterns worked in silk producing shiny satin-like pattern. Blond lace could be natural colored, black or, occasionally, in other colors such as green.

Bombasine. A textile having a twilled appearance with a silk warp and a worsted weft. It was usually black and, because it was lusterless, was often used for mourning.

Book muslin. A cotton fabric with a shiny surface similar to sateen. It was so called because it was often used to face the inside covers of books.

Bouffant. A puff.

Bouillonnée. Puffed or bubbling out.

Brides. Ribbon on bonnets resembling bridle reins.

Brussels sprigs. Floral sprays of Brussels lace, often mounted on machine-made net.

Buckinghamshire. Bobbin lace worked in one piece on a pillow.

Cambric. Very fine thin linen.

Capote. A bonnet with a firm brim and a soft head-shaped crown.

Capuchin. A hood worn by monks; also for out-of-doors use in the 16th, 17th and 18th centuries.

Cashemire (cashmere). A soft woolen fabric with a twill weave originally imported from Kashmir and made of the under hair of Tibetan goats. Later it was imitated in Europe.

Ceinture. Sash, belt, waistband.

Chamois. Soft, pliable leather from chamois (goatlike antelopes) as well as from sheep and goats.

Chemisette. A dickey or fill-in for a low-cut bodice, usually made of fine linen or cotton and often lace trimmed.

Chip. A very coarse straw used especially in women's hats and bonnets.

Circassian cloth. Thin worsted fabric named after Circassia, an area in the Caucasus.

Collerette. Small, usually fancy collar.

Coquelicot. The color poppy red.

Coquings. Shell-shaped trimmings.

Corded point. Point lace (lace made with a needle) and decorated with cording.

Cornette. A bonnet-style day cap, usually made of fine cotton or linen. Worn alone at home or under hats out-of-doors.

Corsage. Bodice or upper part of a women's dress.

Corsage à la soubrette. Bodice in the style of a lady's maid's costume. In the early 19th century, it probably included a corselet like that worn by country girls.

Corsage en [or à la] blouse. Bodice with loose folds or pleats.

Coul (Caul). A cap shaped like the caul or membrane that sometimes covers an infant's head at birth.

Couleur d'oreille d'ours. Color of polyanthus, the oxlip or some variety of narcissus.

Couleur monstre. A green color attributed to monsters or fantastic mythological creatures.

Crape (French crêpe). A thin, crinkled silk, cotton or wool.

Crêpe lisse. A silk gauze without crimping.

Demi-cornette. A sheer day cap that does not fully cover the head and is often worn with a hat or bonnet.

Demi-toilette. A cap or garment worn primarily at home but is not quite a negligee.

Easing. Edge trimming done with puckering, shirring or clipping.

Emarginate. With notched margins.

En bouffants. In puffs or puffed out.

En bouffes. In puffs.

En bride. Ribbons arranged like bridle reins.

En carreaux. In small squares, lozenges or diamond shapes.

En gigot. Sleeves shaped like a leg of mutton with fullness at the shoulder narrowing toward the wrist.

En grandes bouches. Large curls.

En serpent. Serpentine.

En treillis. Like latticework.

En tuyau. With a stem attached.

Étrangère. Unusual, strange, foreign.

Farinet. See À la farinet.

Fichu. Kerchief or small scarf, generally of thin, filmy material, that was worn around the neckline.

Folia peltata. Leaves with stems attached to the underneath part instead of to the edges.

French work. Whitework, including white-on-white embroidery, combined with cut and pieced designs.

Gigot de mouton. Literally, leg of mutton, referring to sleeve shapes which are large at the shoulder and fit closely at the wrist.

Gofre crape. Crinkled, fluted or pleated crepe.

Grenadine. A silk or silk-and-wool mixture woven with an open mesh. Grenadine can be plain or figured.

Gros de Berlin. Ribbed fabric, probably of wool.

Gros de Naples. An Italian silk with corded surface.

Gros des Indes. A heavy silk having a stripe formed transversely to its length.

Honiton. Lace in the Brussels style made in Honiton.

Jaconet (Jacconet). A thin cotton fabric somewhat like muslin.

Jane. Possibly "jean," a sateen with a twill weave.

Jocko. Monkey or ape of great intelligence, hero of numerous 19th-century stage productions, portrayed by a man.

Kerseymere. A fine woolen fabric with a twill weave having a special texture with one third of work threads above and the rest below.

Lappets. Bands or streamers of lace arranged on the sides of the head with ends left pendent.

Leghorn. A plaited Italian wheat straw used in hats.

Letting-in lace. Bands of lace with spaces left open through which ribbons could be threaded.

Levantine. A twilled soft silk with a shiny surface.

Likanian. Term obscure, possibly referring to Lydian- or Phrygian-style cap.

Limeric (Limerick). A glove leather of very fine quality.

Love ribbon. A ribbon of gauze striped with satin.

Lutestring. A glossy silk woven with very fine cording.

Mancherons. Sleeve trimming at the wrists or at the shoulders like epaulettes.

Marabouts (marabou). Soft tail or wing feathers from the marabou stork.

Mull. A very fine, delicate muslin.

Nankeen. A yellowish-brown cotton material.

Navarino. Seaport in southeastern Greece, also called Pylos.

Noeud. A bow or knot.

Parisian mob. A full round cap of fine linen or cotton with a puffed crown and a ruffled border.

Pelerine. A cape-collar or short cape, matching or contrasting.

Pelisse. An outdoor garment such as a coat or cloak.

Plaited. Pleats in cloth; braids in hair.

Pluche (plush). A fabric of silk or wool with a high pile.

Ponceau. Poppy red.

Quadrille feathers. An obscure term, possibly referring to one of four groups of horsemen in a carousel or tournament, each wearing a special colorful costume.

Quilling. Small round pleats sewn lightly to remain open in flute-like folds.

Reticule. Lady's small handbag.

Rouleau (pl. rouleaux). A strip of fabric loosely stuffed into a tube-like shape and used to trim dresses, generally at the hem.

Round gown or dress. A closed one-piece dress.

Ruche. Pleated or closely ruffled strip of lace, net or some soft fabric to be used as trimming.

Sarsnet (sarcenet). A thin silk with a taffeta weave and a slight sheen.

Soie de Londres. Satin or satin-like silk.

Sontag sleeves. Sleeves with fullness confined at intervals by bands. Also called *à la Marie.*

Spanish puffs. Origin of term unclear. Possibly a reference to decorations on Spanish 17th-century costumes.

Spencer. A short jacket, often of contrasting color or material, and ending at a high waistline just below the bust.

Stomacher. A V-shaped inset in the front of the bodice.

Tartarian. In the style of a Tartar's turban.

Thibet cloth. Imitation cashmere made in Paisley, Scotland.

Tippet. A scarf.

Toque. A close-fitting brimless hat.

Toque de Ninon. A toque, possibly in the style of Ninon de Lenclos, a fashionable French lady (1620–1705).

Torsade. A twisted fringe, cord or ribbon used for trimming.

Tucker. A lace or lawn edging used (tucked in) around a low-cut neckline.

Turque. Brilliant soft woolen fabric.

Urling's lace or net. Machine-made lace or net of Urling's Patent Thread, developed in 1817.

Urling's velours natté. Velvet with a twisted nap.

Vandyke (adj. vandyked). A pointed tooth-like border of lace or other material similar to those in the works of Van Dyck (1599–1641).

Velours épingle. Terry velvet.

Velours natté. See Urling's velours natté.

Velours simulé. Simulated velvet.

Wadded. Padded with cotton batting.

Zephyr. A light, very fine, silky cotton.

Zephyrne. Light-weight fabric of silk or wool.